Penguin English
Introducing Discourse Analysis

David Nunan is the Coordinator of Postgraduate Programs in Linguistics and Director of Research and Development at the National Centre for English Language Teaching and Research, Macquarie University, Sydney, Australia. He has worked as a language teacher and lecturer, teacher educator, curriculum developer, materials writer, researcher and consultant in the United Kingdom, Australia, the United States, Thailand, Singapore, Hong Kong, Japan and the Middle East. He is the author of many books and articles on curriculum design and methodology, discourse analysis, teacher education and classroom-based research. His teaching and research interests include curriculum development, language acquisition, discourse analysis and research methods.

David Nunan is Co-Editor of this series.

Ronald Carter is Professor of Modern English Language in the Department of English Studies at the University of Nottingham. He is the author of many books on applied linguistics and was the National Co-ordinator for the LINC (Language in the National Curriculum) project from 1989 to 1992.

Other Titles in the Series

Introducing

DISCOURSE ANALYSIS

David Nunan

Series Editors:
Ronald Carter and David Nunan

PENGUIN
ENGLISH

PENGUIN ENGLISH

Published by the Penguin Group
Penguin Books Ltd, 27 Wrights Lane, London W8 5TZ, England
Penguin Books USA Inc., 375 Hudson Street, New York, New York 10014, USA
Penguin Books Australia Ltd, Ringwood, Victoria, Australia
Penguin Books Canada Ltd, 10 Alcorn Avenue, Toronto, Ontario, Canada M4V 3B2
Penguin Books (NZ) Ltd, 182–190 Wairau Road, Auckland 10, New Zealand

Penguin Books Ltd, Registered Offices: Harmondsworth, Middlesex, England

First published 1993
1 3 5 7 9 10 8 6 4 2

Every endeavour was made to clear permission and the Publisher
would be very happy to hear from the copyright holder, whom
we were unable to trace.

Typeset by Datix International Limited, Bungay, Suffolk
Set in Lasercomp Times Roman
Printed in England by Clays Ltd, St Ives plc

Language is surely as complex a phenomenon as humans have ever wanted to understand, and so far we haven't even come close. We have been retarded in this pursuit by what seems to be a scholarly drive to contract, rather than to expand, the field of vision ... As soon as one looks beyond sentences one finds oneself forced to stop dealing with artificial data concocted to suit one's purposes, and to look instead at language in use.

(Chafe 1990: 21)

The insights provided by work in applied linguistics can be of genuine support to all teachers facing the many complex demands of language learning and teaching. The Penguin English *Introducing Applied Linguistics* series aims to provide short, clear and accessible guides to key topics – helping teachers to keep abreast of this rapidly developing field by explaining recent research and its relevance to common problems and concerns. The books are designed for practical use: they focus on recognizable classroom contexts, suggest problem-solving approaches, and include activities and questions for further study.

Introducing Applied Linguistics presumes an increasing convergence of interest among all English language teachers, and it aims to be relevant both to teachers of English as a second or foreign language and to teachers of English as a mother tongue. As the relationship between linguistics and language teaching continues to develop, so the need grows for books which introduce the field. This series has been developed to meet that need.

The words that appear in **bold** type are
explained in the glossary.

Contents

Contents

Introduction

This book is intended as a basic introduction to discourse and discourse analysis. My principal aim is to introduce you, the reader, to some of the key concepts in the field, and to provide you with an opportunity of exploring these concepts in use.

The book consists of three basic elements. The first of these is the exposition, through which the content or subject matter of the book is presented and discussed. Here, I shall be addressing you, the reader, and providing you with my understanding of the central concepts involved in discourse and discourse analysis. The second element is texts – samples of spoken and written language taken from a wide variety of sources, which will illustrate the major points I wish to make in the book. The final element is a number of activities and projects through which you will be invited to explore discourse and the analysis of discourse within your own context and from your own point of view. Of course, you do not have to do all, or even most, of these activities. However, they will help you to understand the ideas in the book more fully.

Acknowledgements The publishers make grateful acknowledgement to the following for permission to reproduce copyright material: Excerpt from *The Right Stuff* by Tom Wolfe. *Copyright* © 1979 by Tom Wolfe. Reprinted by permission of Farrar, Straus & Giroux, Inc. Reprinted by permission of International Creative Management, Inc. Copyright 1974 by Tom Wolfe; *Dickens* copyright © Peter Ackroyd, 1990, Sinclair-Stephenson; 'Looking Ahead' from *Text*, 10, by W. Chafe, Mouton de Gruyter, a division of Walter de Gruyter & Co., 1990; *Psycholinguistics: a second language perspective*, by E. Hatch, Newbury House, 1983; From 'The impact of interaction on comprehension' by T. Pica, R. Young and C. Doughty, 1987, *TESOL Quarterly*, 21 pages 737–58. Copyright 1987 by T. Pica, R. Young and C. Doughty. Reprinted by permission; *Patrick White: a life* by D. Marr, Jonathon Cape, 1991; 'Genres of Writing' in *Writing in Schools* by F. Christie © Deakin University, 1989; *Spoken and Written Language* by M. A. K. Halliday © Deakin University, 1985, Oxford University Press, 1989; *The Advertiser*, 6 January 1992, Adelaide; Copyright © *The Australian*, 27 December 1991; (p. 25 and p. 72) from *Introducing Linguistics* by David Crystal (Penguin Books, 1992) copyright © David Crystal, 1992. Reproduced by permission of Penguin Books Ltd; Watson 'Why He Failed' from *Newsweek*, 23 December, 1991, Newsweek, Inc. All rights reserved. Reprinted by permission; *Premiere Magazine* for the extract taken from the article 'The Goodfellas';

By permission of the Longman Group UK: *Cohesion in English* by M. A. K. Halliday and R. Hasan, 1976; *Spoken Discourse: a model for analysis* by W. Edmonson, 1981;

By permission of Oxford University Press: *Discourse* by G. Cook, 1989; *A Guide to Orchestral Music* by R. Mordden, 1980; *Patterns of Lexis in Texts* by M. Hoey, 1991; *English in Biological Science* by I. Pearson, 1978; *Towards an Analysis of Discourse: the English used by teachers and pupils* by J. McH. Sinclair and M. Coulthard, 1975; *Teaching Language as communication* by H. G. Widdowson, 1978; *Learning Purpose and Language Use* by H. G. Widdowson, 1983;

By permission of Cambridge University Press: *The Australian English Course Level 2* by D. Nunan, S. Hood and J. Lockwood, 1992; *Studies in Second Language Acquisition* by S. Gass and E. Varonis, 1985; *Structures of Social Action: studies in conversation analysis*, J. M. Atkinson and J. Heritage (eds), 1984; 'Subsequent versions of invitations, offers, requests, and proposals dealing with potential or actual rejection' by J. Davidson in *Structures of Social Action: studies in conversational analysis*, J. M. Atkinson and J. Heritage (eds), 1984; *Discourse Analysis* by G. Brown and G. Yule, 1983; *Teaching the Spoken Language* by G. Brown and B. Yule, 1983; 'Collaborations: constructing shared understandings in a second language classroom' in *Collaborative Language Learning and Teaching* by D. Freeman, 1992; *Pragmatics* by S. Levinson, 1983; *Language Transfer* by T. Odlin, 1989; 'Learner use of strategies in interaction: typology and teachability' by M. Rost and S. Ross in *Language Learning* 41, 1991; *Learning through Interaction* by G. Wells, 1981; *Interchange: English for International communication, Student's Book 1* by J. Richards, J. Hull and S. Proctor, 1990.

For a full list of references, please see page 127.

1   What is discourse analysis?

1.1   What is discourse?

As we shall see, different writers use the term **discourse** in a number of different ways.

ACTIVITY

In order to explore this central question, I should like you to examine the three texts that follow. As you do so, consider which of the extracts make sense and which do not.

1a

BUJUMBURA – It said in a statement on Sunday that 135 people were killed in the capital Bujumbura and surrounding areas and 137 more in the northern provinces of Citiboke and Bubanza. The government said order had been restored but security forces were still on alert for attacks from rebels of the party for the Liberation of the Hutu People. Burundi has said 272 people were killed in clashes between security forces and rebels which flared a week ago in the central African nation.

1b

LIMA – At least 20 members of the Shining Path rebel organization were killed over the weekend by rural vigilantes armed by the government, police said on Monday. Police also said that two people had been killed by rebels – a rancher who had refused to give them money and another man accused of being an informer. The rebels said they planned to enforce what they called an "armed strike" yesterday and today to mark the 57th birthday of Abimael Guzman, the former university professor who founded Shining Path.

1c

At least 14 people died on Saturday after drinking a cheap alcoholic beverage, raising to 20 the number of people killed by the poisonous brew in two days, news reports said. The quake measured 5.7 on the Richter scale and was felt shortly before 10.50 am (0850 GMT) Bucharest radio quoted an official report as saying. Judge Neil Dennison said Robert Phee, 23, a technician on the hit musical "Miss Saigon", was "gripped by the excitement and theatricality" of his eight robberies which netted him 15,000 pounds.

All of the sentences in the above texts come from the same source (*The Nation*, Bangkok, Wednesday 4 December 1991) and from the same column (World Roundup). However, in terms of their **coherence**, the texts are very different. In fact, many readers dispute that text 1c is a text at all.

What knowledge do we need in order to make sense of these extracts? In the first place, we need to understand the grammar and vocabulary used in constructing the sentences which make up each text. However, we need more than this, because, taken by themselves, each of the sentences in the three extracts is grammatically unexceptional, so it is obviously not the grammar that accounts for the oddity of the text. Of course, the sentences that make up a text need to be grammatical, but grammatical sentences alone will not ensure that the text itself makes sense.

In addition to the structure and meaning of the individual sentences, we need to know how the sentences relate to each other. The sentences in text 1c do not seem to relate to each other at all. While the sentences in text 1a do seem to relate to each other in some way, the arrangement appears to be rather odd. In the first sentence, for example, there does not seem to be any way of determining what *It* refers to.

1.1.1   Text-forming devices

It is clear that, in addition to sentence-level knowledge, the reader also needs to be able to interpret the sentences in relation to one another.

ACTIVITY

In order to consider in greater detail this issue of the interconnections between the sentences in a piece of discourse, consider the following sentences which have been taken from Hoey (1983). The sentences originally formed a coherent passage, but have been jumbled up. See whether you can determine the original order.

1d
(*1*) *In England, however, the tungsten-tipped spikes would tear the thin tarmac surfaces of our roads to pieces as soon as the protective layer of snow or ice melted.*
(2) *Road maintenance crews try to reduce the danger of skidding by scattering sand upon the road surface.*
(3) *We therefore have to settle for the method described above as the lesser of two evils.*
(4) *Their spikes grip the icy surfaces and enable the motorist to corner safely where non-spiked tyres would be disastrous.*
(5) *Its main drawback is that if there are fresh snowfalls the whole process has to be repeated, and if the snowfalls continue, it becomes increasingly ineffective in providing some kind of grip for tyres.*
(6) *These tyres prevent most skidding and are effective in the extreme weather conditions as long as the roads are regularly cleared of loose snow.*
(7) *Such a measure is generally adequate for our very brief snowfalls.*
(8) *Whenever there is snow in England, some of the country roads may have black ice.*

3

(9) *In Norway, where there may be snow and ice for nearly seven months of the year, the law requires that all cars be fitted with special spiked tyres.*

(10) *Motorists coming suddenly upon stretches of black ice may find themselves skidding off the road.*

(Hoey 1983: 4)

The order in which these sentences originally appeared was as follows: 8–10–2–7–5–9–6–4–1–3. How close were you to the original? Go over the sentences again, and underline the words and phrases that were important in helping you to reorder the sentences.

When over 200 undergraduate students were asked to carry out this sentence reordering task, the results demonstrated close agreement as to what was an acceptable ordering. In addition, when students did provide an order which differed from the original, the differences were limited to only a small number of variations.

What is it about the sentences which brings about this close agreement? According to Hoey, it is the existence within the sentences of certain **text-forming devices**: '. . . the majority of the sentences in the discourse connect unambiguously with their neighbours in one of two ways. Some are connected by means of anaphoric (that is, backward referring) devices of several kinds (eg such, its, this), the remainder by simple repetition.' (Hoey 1983: 6)

The text-forming devices are listed below. How do these compare with the words and phrases you underlined in the original sentences?

Sentence 8:	*black ice*	
Sentence 10:	*black ice*	*skidding*
Sentence 2:	*skidding*	*scattering sand on the road surface*
Sentence 7:	*such a measure*	
Sentence 5:	*Its*	
Sentence 9:	*tyres*	
Sentence 6:	*these tyres*	
Sentence 4:	*Their*	*spikes*

how to def. discourse - they what it is ?
a say what it's not.
What is discourse analysis?

Sentence 1:   *spikes*
Sentence 3:   *method described above*

From studies such as these, it has been argued that the difference between coherent pieces of discourse (such as 1b) and disconnected sentences (such as 1c) is to be found in the words and phrases that connect each sentence with one or more of the sentences that come before it.

However, that is not the end of the story. As we shall see, in addition to what we might call 'linguistic knowledge' (that is, knowledge of how sentences are formed internally, and combined with each other externally), there is also 'non-linguistic knowledge' (that is, knowledge of the subject matter or content of the text in question). Later, we shall consider evidence which suggests that subject matter knowledge plays an important part in enabling the reader (or listener) to interpret texts. We shall also look at the views of a number of linguists who disagree with the idea that it is the connecting words and phrases that create discourse.

From what I have already said, it would seem that discourse can be defined as a stretch of language consisting of several sentences which are perceived as being related in some way. In later sections, we shall see that sentences can be related, not only in terms of the ideas they share, but also in terms of the jobs they perform within the discourse – that is, in terms of their **functions**.

What does a text e.g. distinguish from discourse? sentences p. 4 Mills

1.2   Discourse versus text

So far, I have used the terms 'discourse' and 'text' as though they are synonyms. It is time to look at these terms a little more closely. Consider the following statements, which have been extracted from a number of different sources.

1. '**discourse**   A continuous stretch of (especially spoken) language larger than a sentence, often constituting a coherent unit, such as a sermon, argument, joke or narrative.' (Crystal 1992: 25)

2. 'text   A piece of naturally occurring spoken, written, or signed discourse identified for purposes of analysis. It is often a language unit with a definable communicative function, such as a conversation, a poster.' (Crystal 1992: 72)

3. 'We shall use text as a technical term, to refer to the verbal record of a communicative act.' (Brown and Yule 1983a: 6)

4. 'discourse: stretches of language perceived to be meaningful, unified, and purposive.' (Cook 1989: 156)

5. 'text: a stretch of language interpreted formally, without context.' (Cook 1989: 158)

From these extracts it can be seen that there is disagreement about the meaning of these two terms. For some writers, the terms seem to be used almost interchangeably; for others, discourse refers to language in context. All, however, seem to agree that both text and discourse need to be defined in terms of meaning, and that coherent texts/pieces of discourse are those that form a meaningful whole.

Let us examine some of the claims and assumptions in the quotes.

ASSERTION: the terms 'text' and 'discourse' are interchangeable. While some commentators appear to use the terms interchangeably, others draw a clear distinction between them. Some people argue that discourse is language in action, while a text is the written record of that interaction. According to this view, discourse brings together language, the individuals producing the language, and the context within which the language is used. Yet other linguists tend to avoid using the term 'discourse' altogether, preferring the term 'text' for all recorded instances of language in use.

In this book, I shall use the term text to refer to any written record of a communicative event. The event itself may involve oral language (for example, a sermon, a casual conversation, a shopping transaction) or written language (for example, a poem, a newspaper advertisement, a wall poster, a shopping list, a novel). I shall reserve the term discourse to refer to the interpretation of the communicative event in context. In this book, I shall discuss aspects of both **text analysis** and **discourse analysis** – that is, I shall deal with both the linguistic analysis of texts and an interpretation of those texts.

ASSERTION: discourse analysis involves the study of language in use. The assertion here is that the analysis of discourse involves the analysis of language in use – compared with an analysis of the structural properties of language divorced from their communicative functions (which Cook (1989), among others, refers to as text analysis). All linguists – from the phonetician, through the grammarian, to the discourse analyst – are concerned with identifying regularities and patterns in language. However, in the case of the discourse analyst, the ultimate aim of this analytical work is both to show and to interpret the relationship between these regularities and the meanings and purposes expressed through discourse.

ASSERTION: a text or piece of discourse consists of more than one sentence and the sentences combine to form a meaningful whole. The notion that a text should form a 'meaningful whole' – that is, convey a complete message – is commonsensical, although it is not always easy to determine where one text ends and another begins. The notion that a text should consist of more than one sentence or utterance is arguable. Consider the following: *STOP!*, *GO!*, *WAIT!*, *OUCH!* Each of these utterances consists of a single word. However, they are, nonetheless, complete texts in their own right. Each conveys a coherent message, and can therefore be said to form a meaningful whole. I believe that, given an appropriate context, many words can function as complete texts.

1.2.1 Context

From what I have said in the previous section, it is obvious that context is an important concept in discourse analysis. Context refers to the situation giving rise to the discourse, and within which

7

the discourse is embedded. There are two different types of context. The first of these is the linguistic context – the language that surrounds or accompanies the piece of discourse under analysis. The second is the non-linguistic or experiential context within which the discourse takes place. Non-linguistic contexts include: the type of communicative event (for example, joke, story, lecture, greeting, conversation); the topic; the purpose of the event; the setting, including location, time of day, season of year and physical aspects of the situation (for example, size of room, arrangement of furniture); the participants and the relationships between them; and the **background knowledge** and assumptions underlying the communicative event.

1.3 Spoken versus written language

Although spoken language emerged before written language, written texts are much more than merely 'talk written down'. According to Halliday (1985b), writing emerged in societies as a result of cultural changes which created new communicative needs. These needs could not be readily met by the spoken language. In particular, with the emergence of cultures based on agriculture rather than hunting and gathering, people needed permanent records which could be referred to over and over again. This led to the emergence of a new form of language – writing.

Written language does, in fact, perform a similar range of broad functions to those performed by spoken language – that is, it is used to get things done, to provide information and to entertain. However, the contexts for using written language are very different from those in which spoken language is used. For example, in the case of information, written language is used to communicate with others who are removed in time and space, or for those occasions on which a permanent or semi-permanent record is required. While most people in other cities or countries could be communicated with by telephone, certain types of message are more appropriate in written form – for example, postcard greetings to family and friends.

Halliday (1985b) suggests that written language is used for action (for example, public signs, product labels, television and radio guides, bills, menus, telephone directories, ballot papers, computer manuals); for information (for example, newspapers, current affairs magazines, advertisements, political pamphlets); and for entertainment (for example, comic strips, fiction books, poetry and drama, newspaper features, film subtitles). These different purposes will be reflected in the characteristics of the texts themselves: letters have different characteristics from newspaper editorials, which have different characteristics from poems, and so on. As we shall see when we consider the concept of **genre**, these differences can be observed within the sentence at the level of grammar, and beyond the sentence at the level of text structure.

The differences between spoken and written modes are not absolute, and the characteristics that we tend to associate with written language can sometimes occur in spoken language and vice versa. This means that some spoken texts will be more like written texts than others, while some written texts will be more like spoken texts than others.

ACTIVITY

What are some of the things which make text 1e different from text 1f?

1e
Annie,
Gone to the deli for milk. Back in a tick.
Go in and make yourself at home.
– Theo
(Author's data)

1f

At times one's preoccupation with averages can cause one to lose sight of the fact that many of the most important workaday decisions are based on considerations of the extremes rather than on the middle of a distribution.

(Author's data)

Most native speakers would recognize 1e as being more like spoken language than 1f, even though 1e is a written text and text 1f could conceivably be spoken.

1.3.1 Grammar

Despite this overlap, written language has certain features that are generally not shared by the spoken language. Linguistically, written language tends to consist of clauses that are internally complex, whereas with spoken language the complexity exists in the ways in which clauses are joined together. This is illustrated in the following extracts – 1g being the written text and 1h being the spoken one.

1g

Like Vincent d'Indy, a disciple of Cesar Frank, Chausson shares with them a dreamy, even idle poetry, sumptuous but precise orchestration, and an energy that is intimate rather than powerful, ascetic rather than importunate.

(Mordden 1980: 292)

1h

This morning Associate Professor Dean Wolfe will talk about the science of music at half-past eleven, and we'll hear some fascinating things such as musicians playing music backwards – but most of it will be played forwards!

(Author's data)

We can see that the written text, 1g, seems to have more information packed into it. This text contains only one main clause, in contrast with the spoken text in which there are several clauses chained together in an additive fashion. In a sense, spoken language is 'unedited'. If the speaker above had had the opportunity to present the same content in written form, he may have produced something along the following lines:

1i

This morning at half-past eleven, Associate Professor Dean Wolfe will present a programme entitled 'The Science of Music', in which the listener will experience a number of fascinating things, including music played backwards – although most will be played forwards!

1.3.2 Lexical density

Spoken and written language also differ in the ratio of **content words** to **grammatical** or **function words**. (Content or lexical words include nouns and verbs, while grammatical words include such things as prepositions, pronouns and articles.) The number of lexical or content words per clause is referred to as **lexical density**. In the following example, from Halliday (1985b), there are twelve content words in a single clause, and it therefore has a lexical density of twelve.

1j

The use of this method of control unquestionably leads to safer and faster trains running in the most adverse weather conditions.

A spoken version of the above text might be as follows:

1k

You can control the trains this way
and if you do that
you can be quite sure
that they'll be able to run more safely and more quickly
than they would otherwise
no matter how bad the weather gets

In 1k, there are ten content words (*control, trains, way, sure, run, safely, quickly, bad, weather, gets*) distributed between five clauses, which gives the text a lexical density of two.

The density of written language is also reinforced by the tendency to create nouns from verbs. Examples of this process are as follows:

SPOKEN

Good writers reflect on what they write.

WRITTEN

Reflection is a characteristic of good writers.

Halliday (1985b) calls this process of turning verbs into nouns **grammatical metaphor**. He suggests that the spoken forms are in a sense more basic than the written forms and that, in writing, by turning verbs into nouns, we have altered the normal state of events. In other words, processes or functions which in the grammatical system of English would normally be represented as verbs have been transformed into 'things' and represented as nouns. It is this transformation which led Halliday to use the term 'metaphor'.

These linguistic differences between spoken and written language are not absolutes. As I have already pointed out, some written texts share many of the characteristics of spoken texts, and vice versa. Ultimately, the linguistic shape of the text will be determined by a range of factors relating to the context and purpose for which it was produced in the first place.

ACTIVITY

Study the following written text. Can you identify any ways in which its linguistic features are determined by the context and purpose for which it was produced?

11

1.3.3   Situation

Spoken and written language also differ in terms of the demands that they make on the listener or reader. With written language there is no common situation, as there is in face-to-face interaction. The situation therefore has to be inferred from the text. In addition, the words themselves must carry all of the shades of meaning which in face-to-face interaction can be conveyed by non-verbal behaviour. Then again, there is no opportunity for the readers to signal that they do not understand. The writer must make assumptions about the reader's state of knowledge. If incorrect assumptions are made, then communication may be seriously impaired. Finally, as we have already seen, written language is more densely packed with information than spoken language. This can create problems for the immature reader, for individuals who are reading in a second or foreign language, or for those reading about unfamiliar concepts.

ACTIVITY

Study the following conversation, which has been taken from Christie (1989: 51) and see if you can work out what it is about.

1m
J.   *Oh, this is beautiful!*
R.   *Oh, yes, that's right.*
J.   *Is that how you . . . you wanted it hard boiled, didn't you?*
R.   *Yes, that's what I call hard.*
J.   *Well, do you want to have this one?*
R.   *No, you have that one, 'cause this one must be harder, mustn't it?*
J.   *Doesn't necessarily follow.*
F.   *Yes, surely it . . . oh, you're right . . . it doesn't.*
J.   *Depends which one went in first.*
R.   *Yes, you're right, well look, in a minute we'll know.*

This extract is from a lengthy conversation between three friends on holiday who are cooking eggs for breakfast.

ACTIVITY

Now consider a written account of the conversation. As you do, make a note of the differences between the two extracts.

1n

Fran, Jim and Ros went away together one Easter holiday weekend. They spent the first night in a holiday cabin they had rented. In the morning, having slept well they got up and prepared breakfast in the tiny kitchen.

Ros and Jim both decided to have a boiled egg, while Fran, who didn't like eggs, settled simply for a toasted Easter bun and coffee. The breakfast preparations proceeded very cordially, though some confusion was caused by the fact that Ros placed the two eggs in the boiling water at different times. Subsequently, she was not able to tell which egg had been in the water longer, though she particularly wanted a hard-boiled egg herself.

Ros removed one egg from the saucepan in which it was cooking and gave it to Jim who discovered it was quite hard. Ros concluded that the other egg must be hard too, though as Jim pointed out, she had no reason to believe this, since there was no way of knowing which egg had been placed in the water first. The matter was only resolved when the removal of the second egg from the water revealed that it was as hard as the first egg.

These two texts illustrate some of the differences between spoken and written language which I have already discussed. The language in text 1m accompanies a sequence of actions in context, whereas text 1n is written for an unknown audience which is distant in time and place. In text 1m, there are numerous references to things outside of the text itself. These are not explicitly identified but are referred to by words and phrases such as *this, it, that, this one, that one, it* etc. In text 1n, because the writer must construct a context for the interaction, objects, people, actions etc. are named.

The need to be explicit leads to another major difference – that of lexical density. In fact, there are over twice as many content words in 1n as in 1m. You can check this by going back to the text and underlining the content words.

1.4 Types of discourse

We can classify discourse types in terms of the communicative job they are doing.

ACTIVITY

Study the following pieces of discourse and see whether you can categorize them according to the job they appear to be doing.

1o

A: *It's a worry isn't it?*

B: *What?*

A: *Your money (yes) organizing your money affairs.*

B: *tis . . . A big worry.*

C: *Mmm*

B: *I've got to manage my money to look after myself in my old age.*

A: *You're in it.*

B: *What?*

A: *You're in it – you're in your old age.*

B: *I might live for another ten years. Be . . .*

C: *Be a bloody miracle. [laughter]*

B: *What? What did she say?*

A: *Be a miracle – after the life you've led. If you'd led a nice sedentary existence and hadn't drunk or smoked you might've been able to look forward to a telegram from the Queen.*

C: *Be a thrill!*

A: A big thrill.
(Author's data)

1p
A: Where do you keep your detergents and stuff?
B: Next aisle – middle row of shelves.
A: Oh, yeah, got it. Is this the smallest you've got?
B: Yeah, what'd you . . .
A: . . . it's a bit
B: Mmm.– the Down Earth brand's on special.
A: OK, right . . . Mmm three fifty-nine – still not cheap.
B: Well, that's the smallest they made I'm afraid.
(Author's data)

1q
This is Dr Graham Lowe. We are closed for the weekend, but if you want to contact me after hours, you will need to do two things. Firstly, after the beep at the end of my message, leave your full name and telephone number. Then, you'll need to hang up, and then dial my pager activating number which is 017331923 which will make my pager beep. That's 017331923. I will then ring through as soon as possible to get your message, and then I'll ring you. We'll be open as usual on Monday morning at 8.45 am. Beep!
(Nunan, Hood and Lockwood 1991)

1r
A: Pauline arrived today with amoebic dysentery . . . she
B: Amoebic
A: She got amoebic dysentery in India with . . . and so did Phil . . . this is their celebration trip – their reunion – their you know
C: Who's Phil?
A: Phil Bryant . . . her boyfriend
C: Ahhh
B: Mmmm
A: After her MA, when they got together again – met in India for

this great trip and then they both contracted amoebic dysentery . . . spent some time in India sick as they could be – then were . . . flew back to Sydney where they both remained very ill but Pauline got a bit better and now she's had a relapse and she's come . . . she was coming today . . .

B: *Mmmm*

C: *Ahhh*

A: *That's all a bit nasty*

B: *You often do with amoebic dysentery*

A: *Yeah*

N: *You said something . . .*

B: *You've got to be fed intravenously or something and starve it out*

A: *I thought once you had an amoeba you never got rid of it*

C: *Starve them out*

B: *No you can starve it out . . . by having no food go into your stomach for a week or something*

(Author's data)

One way in which the texts could be divided up is into dialogue and monologue. Another division would be into those that are basically transactional in nature, and those that are basically interpersonal. **Transactional language** is that which occurs when the participants are concerned with the exchange of goods and services. **Interpersonal language**, on the other hand, occurs when the speakers are less concerned with the exchange of goods and services, than with socializing. If we follow this distinction, we will group texts 1o and 1r together under the heading of interpersonal, and texts 1p and 1q together under the heading of transactional. This distinction – between language which is used to get goods and services, and language which is used to fulfil a social purpose – is a common one in the literature (see, for example, Brown and Yule 1983a). This is not to say that a given text will only exhibit one or other of these functions. Many interactions that are essentially transactional in nature will also exhibit social functions, while essentially social interactions can contain transactional elements. This is demonstrated in the following conversation in which there are both transactional and interpersonal functions.

1s

A: *G'day.*

B: *Hi.*

A: *Nice day.*

B: *Yeah. Rohan been in yet?*

A: *Dunno – I've just started. The usual?*

B: *Ta.*

(Author's data)

These two major functional categories do not exhaust the possibilities of course. Consider the function of the following text.

1t

the land drops away and with it
the last worry disagreement uncertainty

this
is the freedom of the stop-over the
not being able to understand the
not having to explain
the freedom of strangers

yet at the back of the mind

a night thick with stars whose
warm breeze stirs the dust like
a dark blanket and all around are voices

the original city of man
(Cataldi 1990)

Here, the primary purpose is neither to secure goods and services, nor to 'oil the wheels of social life'. Rather, it fulfils an expressive or aesthetic function. This aesthetic function is a third major purpose for which people use language.

PROJECT

Record and transcribe a 5–10 minute conversation between two or three people. What can you say about the following characteristics?
— topic
— purpose or function
— setting
— participants and their relationship
— message form
— message content

SUMMARY

- Two key terms in this book are 'text' and discourse'. Text refers to a written or taped record of a piece of communication, whereas discourse refers to the piece of communication in context.
- Text analysis is the study of the formal linguistic devices that distinguish a text from random sentences.
- Discourse analysts also study these text-forming devices. However, they do so with reference to the purposes and functions for which the discourse was produced, as well as the context within which the discourse was created. Their ultimate aim is to show how the linguistic elements enable language users to communicate in context.
- In considering the purposes for which language is used, we can distinguish between 'transactional' language, which is language used to obtain goods and services, and 'interpersonal' language, which is language used for socializing.
- Another important distinction is between spoken and written language. Both modes have evolved to serve different communicative purposes, and these different purposes are reflected in the discourse itself.

2   Linguistic elements in discourse

2.1   Cohesion

In chapter 1, we saw that coherent texts – that is, sequences of sentences or utterances which seem to 'hang together' – contain what are called text-forming devices. These are words and phrases which enable the writer or speaker to establish relationships across sentence or utterance boundaries, and which help to tie the sentences in a text together. In this section I shall look at these text-forming devices in greater detail.

The most comprehensive description and analysis of these devices is to be found in Halliday and Hasan (1976). They identified five different types of **cohesion: reference, substitution, ellipsis, conjunction** and **lexical cohesion**. In Halliday (1985a) these have been further refined and the five categories have been reduced to four, with substitution being seen as a sub-category of ellipsis.

2.1.1   Referential cohesion

If a single sentence is taken out of context and presented in isolation, it is likely to contain elements that are difficult, if not impossible, to interpret. Consider the following fragment: *He is near the end of the* Cape Fear *shoot, in front of a grocer's stand just outside Fort Lauderdale, Florida . . . He used to have Armani make his jeans, but he felt guilty wearing them.*

Who is this mysterious figure on the outskirts of Fort Lauderdale, who suffers guilt over the wearing of jeans by a particular designer? The item *he* is uninterpretable. However, if we have access to the context in which the sentence appears, the question is quite straightforward.

2a

Martin Scorsese is killing time, waiting for the sun to go behind a cloud so the next shot will match the last one. He is near the end of the Cape Fear *shoot, in front of a grocer's stand just outside Fort Lauderdale, Florida. With him are Nick Nolte, Jessica Lange and Juliette Lewis, playing a married couple and their daughter fleeing from a psycho. Scorsese's hand rarely leaves the side pocket of his custom-made jeans, where he works his watch chain like worry beads. He used to have Armani make his jeans, but he felt guilty wearing them.*
(Premiere Magazine)

Anaphoric and cataphoric reference

There are two different ways in which reference items can function within a text. They can function in an anaphoric way. Or they can function in a cataphoric way. In text 2a the words *Martin Scorsese, he, him, his, he, his, he, his* and *he* all refer to a single individual whose identity is established in the opening sentence. The subsequent items can only be interpreted with reference to the initial phrase of this first sentence. This type of device is known as **anaphoric reference**. Anaphoric reference points the reader or listener 'backwards' to a previously mentioned entity, process or state of affairs. **Cataphoric reference** points the reader or listener forward – it draws us further into the text in order to identify the elements to which the reference items refer. Authors sometimes use cataphoric reference for dramatic effect, as in the following extract:

2b

Within five minutes, or ten minutes, no more than that, three of the others had called her on the telephone to ask her if she had heard that something had happened out there.

"Jane, this is Alice. Listen, I just got a call from <u>Betty</u>, and she said she heard something's happened out there. Have you heard anything?" That was the way they phrased it, call after call. She picked up the telephone and began relaying this same message to some of the others.
(Wolfe 1979)

Personal, demonstrative and comparative reference

Halliday and Hasan (1976) identify three sub-types of referential cohesion – personal, demonstrative and comparative. These various devices enable the writer or speaker to make multiple references to people and things within a text. Examples of each type follow. (The first part of the referential relationship is underlined, the second is in bold.)

PERSONAL REFERENCE

Personal reference items, such as those in text 2a, are expressed through pronouns and determiners. They serve to identify individuals and objects that are named at some other point in the text.
<u>*Mikhail Gorbachev*</u> *didn't have to change the world.* **He** *could have chosen to rule much as his predecessors did.*
(*The Bulletin*, 24 December 1991)

DEMONSTRATIVE REFERENCE

Demonstrative reference is expressed through determiners and adverbs. These items can represent a single word or phrase, or much longer chunks of text – ranging across several paragraphs or even several pages.
<u>*Recognizing that his country had to change, Gorbachev could have become a cautious modernizer in the Chinese fashion, promoting economic reform and sponsoring new technology while holding firm against political change.*</u> **This** did not happen.

COMPARATIVE REFERENCE

Comparative reference is expressed through adjectives and adverbs and serves to compare items within a text in terms of identity or similarity.

A: *Would you like these seats?*

B: *No, as a matter of fact, I'd like* **the other seats**.

ACTIVITY

How many instances of referential cohesion can you find in the following conversation?

2c

A: *That's a funny looking bottle.*

B: *Yes, it is, isn't it. It's beautiful. Beer's nice too.*

A: *Oh, gosh, that's lovely. Where'd you buy that?*

B: *Oh, there's a little bottle shop in the city called the Wine . . . City Wines. Maybe we'll go there tomorrow and have a look.*

A: *That'd be good. I'd love to keep this bottle. Wish we could keep it.*

(Author's data)

2.1.2 Substitution and ellipsis

In their 1976 work on cohesion, Halliday and Hasan deal with substitution and ellipsis separately, although they do point out that these two types of cohesion are essentially the same. Ellipsis is described as a form of substitution in which the original item is replaced by zero. In a later publication, Halliday (1985a) combines substitution and ellipsis into a single category.

Substitution

There are three types of subsitution – nominal, verbal and clausal. Examples of each type follow.

NOMINAL SUBSTITUTION

There are some new <u>tennis balls</u> in the bag. These ones've lost their bounce.

VERBAL SUBSTITUTION

A: Annie says you <u>drink too much</u>.
B: So <u>do</u> you!

CLAUSAL SUBSTITUTION

A: Is it <u>going to rain</u>?
B: I think <u>so</u>.

In each of these examples, part of the preceding text has been replaced by *ones*, *do*, and *so* respectively. These words can only be interpreted in relation to what has gone before.

Ellipsis

Ellipsis occurs when some essential structural element is omitted from a sentence or clause and can only be recovered by referring to an element in the preceding text. Consider the following discourse fragment and comprehension question.

Mary: I prefer the green.

Question: Select the correct alternative: Mary prefers the green:
(a) hat, (b) dress, (c) shoes.

As it stands, the question is impossible to answer. However, if we know what was said before, it becomes relatively straightforward.

Sylvia: I like the blue hat.
Mary: I prefer the green.

As with substitution, there are three types of ellipsis – nominal, verbal and clausal. Examples of each type follow. (The point at which material has been omitted from the second sentence of each text is marked by (0).) In each instance, see whether you can identify the material that has been left out.

NOMINAL ELLIPSIS

My kids play an awful lot of sport. Both (0) are incredibly energetic.

VERBAL ELLIPSIS

A: Have you been working?
B: Yes, I have (0).

CLAUSAL ELLIPSIS

A: Why'd you only set three places? Paul's staying for dinner, isn't he?
B: Is he? He didn't tell me (0).

2.1.3 Conjunction

Conjunction differs from reference, substitution and ellipsis in that it is not a device for reminding the reader of previously mentioned entities, actions and states of affairs. In other words, it is not what linguists call an anaphoric relation. However, it is a cohesive device because it signals relationships that can only be fully understood through reference to other parts of the text. There are four different types of conjunction – temporality, causality, addition and adversity. Examples of each type follow.

ADVERSATIVE

I'm afraid I'll be home late tonight. However, I won't have to go in until late tomorrow.
I quite like being chatted up when I'm sitting in a bar having a drink. On the other hand, I hate it if . . . you know . . . if the guy starts to make a nuisance of himself.

(The relationships signalled by *however* and *on the other hand* are adversative because the information in the second sentence of each text moderates or qualifies the information in the first.)

ADDITIVE

From a marketing viewpoint, the popular tabloid encourages the reader to read the whole page instead of choosing stories. And isn't that what any publisher wants?

(Here *And* signals the presentation of additional information.)

TEMPORAL

Brick tea is a blend that has been compressed into a cake. It is taken mainly by the minority groups in China. First, it is ground to a dust. Then it is usually cooked in milk.

(Temporal relationships exist when the events in a text are related in terms of the timing of their occurrence.)

CAUSAL

Chinese tea is becoming increasingly popular in restaurants, and even in coffee shops. This is because of the growing belief that it has several health-giving properties.

(In this type of conjunction, the relationship is one of cause and consequence.)

At this point, I should like to refer briefly to a point that will be dealt with in greater detail in chapter 3: the cohesive devices themselves do not create the relationships in the text; what they do is to make the relationships explicit. In fact, most clauses in a text can relate to some others without the relationship being explicitly signalled to the listener or reader by a conjunction. There is a temporal relationship in both the two following texts (from Martin 1981a), but this is only explicitly marked in the second text.

1. *John came in. He sat down.*
2. *John came in. Then he sat down.*

. . . the conjunction 'then' does not create the temporal relation. For a speaker to produce text 1, and for a listener to understand it, it is essential that a temporal relation is recognised. The simple juxtaposition of the clauses in 1 is sufficient to signal the relation. What the 'then' in 2 does is put a 'stamp' on the relation in question, making it explicit to the listener that one action happened after the other. (Martin 1981a: 1)

ACTIVITY

How many cohesive relationships can you identify in the following text?

2d

Plants characteristically synthesise complex organic substances from simple inorganic raw materials. In green plants, the energy of this process is sunlight. The plants can use this energy because they possess the green pigment chlorophyll. Photosynthesis or 'light synthesis', is a 'self feeding', or autotrophic process.

Animals on the other hand, must obtain complex organic substances by eating plants and other animals. The reason for this is that they lack chlorophyll. Among these 'other feeders' or phagotrophs, are 'liquid feeders' or osmotrophs. Whereas phagotrophic organisms take in solid and often living food, osmotrophic ones absorb or suck up liquid food. This is usually from dead or rotting organisms.
(Pearson 1978)

2.1.4 Lexical cohesion

Lexical cohesion occurs when two words in a text are semantically related in some way – in other words, they are related in terms of their meaning. In Halliday and Hasan (1976), the two major categories of lexical cohesion are **reiteration** and **collocation**.

Reiteration

Reiteration includes repetition, synonym or near synonym, super-ordinate, and general word. Examples of each type follow. The second underlined word or phrase in each of the texts refers back to the previously mentioned entity. Reiteration thus fulfils a similar semantic function to cohesive reference.

REPETITION

What we lack in a <u>newspaper</u> is what we should get. In a word, a 'popular' <u>newspaper</u> may be the winning ticket.

SYNONYM

You could try reversing the car up the <u>slope</u>. The <u>incline</u> isn't all that steep.

SUPERORDINATE

<u>*Pneumonia*</u> *has arrived with the cold and wet conditions. <u>The illness</u> is striking everyone from infants to the elderly.*

GENERAL WORD

A: Did you try the <u>steamed buns</u>?
B: Yes, I didn't like the <u>things</u> much.

Collocation

Collocation can cause major problems for discourse analysis because it includes all those items in a text that are semantically related. In some cases this makes it difficult to decide for certain whether a cohesive relationship exists or not. In extract 2d, we could say that the following items are examples of lexical collocation because they all belong to the scientific field of biology: *plants . . . synthesise . . . organic . . . inorganic . . . green plants . . . energy . . . sunlight . . . plants . . . energy . . . green pigment . . . chlorophyll . . . photosynthesis . . . light synthesis . . . self feeding . . . autotrophic.*

Most linguists who have written about cohesion admit that lexical collocation is a problem, and some refuse to deal with it because of this. Martin (1981b: 1) points out that, while there are problems in defining collocation, 'its contribution to coherence in text is so significant that it cannot be ignored'. The problems arise because collocation is expressed through open rather than closed class items. 'Closed' lexical items include all grammatical words – such as pronouns, conjunctions and prepositions – membership of which is finite. In contrast, there is no limit to the items that can be used to express collocation. This means that it is difficult to establish sets of regularly co-occurring words and phrases.

An additional problem is the fact that many **lexical relationships** are text- as well as context-bound. This means that words and phrases that are related in one text may not be related in another. For example, the words *neighbour* and *scoundrel* are not related at all. However, in the following text they are synonyms.

My neighbour has just let one of his trees fall into my garden.
And the scoundrel refuses to pay for the damage he has caused.

Given this text-bound nature of many lexical relationships, it is impossible to develop a finite list of relatable lexical items in English. However, despite its problematic nature, lexical cohesion is, in many ways, the most interesting of all the cohesive categories. The **background knowledge** of the reader or listener plays a more obvious role in the perception of lexical relationships than in the perception of other types of cohesion. Collocational patterns, for example, will only be perceived by someone who knows something about the subject at hand. The text-bound nature of many lexical relations, and the role of the language user in perceiving these, creates a problem for the linguist concerned with providing a semantic account of lexical cohesion.

One problem that arises in analysing these relations in text has to do with how many 'steps' away an item can be in a word class and still contribute to cohesion. For example, *rose* and *flower* seem more closely related than *rose* and *plant*; and though one would accept a relationship between *mosquito* and *insect*, one wonders about *mosquito* and *animal*. Are the latter items too many steps apart in the class to be related?

As I have already suggested, text- or context-free word classes can only ever be partial, and the test of whether many items are cohesive or not will be determined by the particular text in which they occur. In addition, our ability to identify collocational relationships in a text will depend on our background knowledge – that is, on our familiarity with the content of a text.

Hoey (1991) argues that lexical cohesion is the single most important form of cohesion, accounting for something like forty per cent of cohesive ties in texts. His work is too complex to deal with in any detail here. However, it is worth looking briefly at his central idea.

Hoey argues that various lexical relationships between the different sentences making up a text provide a measure of the cohesiveness of the text. The centrality and importance to the text of any particular sentence within the text will be determined by the number of lexical connections that sentence has to other sentences in the text. He illustrates this point with an analysis of the following text.

2e

DRUG CRAZED GRIZZLIES

A drug known to produce violent reactions in humans has been used for sedating grizzly bears Ursus arctos *in Montana, USA, according to a report in* The New York Times. *After one bear, known to be a peaceable animal, killed and ate a camper in an unprovoked attack, scientists discovered it had been tranquillized 11 times with phencyclidine or 'angel dust', which causes hallucinations and sometimes gives the user an irrational feeling of destructive power. Many wild bears have become 'garbage junkies', feeding from dumps around human developments. To avoid potentially dangerous clashes between them and humans, scientists are trying to rehabilitate the animals by drugging them and releasing them in uninhabited areas. Although*

some biologists deny that the mind-altering drug was responsible for uncharacteristic behaviour of this particular bear, no research has been done into the effects of giving grizzly bears or other mammals repeated doses of phencyclidine.
(*BBC Wildlife*, 1984, 2, 3: 160)

Hoey's analysis consists, first, of counting the number of repetition links between the different sentences in the text. Sentence 1 has four links with the sentences 2, 3, 4 and 5. These are listed below:

1. *produce   humans   used   sedating grizzly bears*
2. *bear   tranquillized   user*
3. *bears   human*
4. *them   humans   animals   drugging*
5. *drug   responsible for   grizzly bears*

(Note that while *known to* appears in both sentences 1 and 2, they are not treated as repetition as they refer to different events.)

Using this procedure, it is possible to begin to identify the number of connections between each of the sentences in a text.

The different types of cohesion discussed in this section are set out in the figure opposite.

It is important for language teachers to have some understanding of cohesion and the ways in which it makes textual relationships explicit. As we shall see in chapter 4, learning to read and write involves developing control of these various devices, and it has been shown that young children can benefit from explicit instruction in using them.

2.2   Information structure

In this section, we shall examine the ways in which information is organized within and beyond the sentence. We shall see that the way in which information is arranged within a sentence will be affected by the pattern of the sentences within the text as a whole.

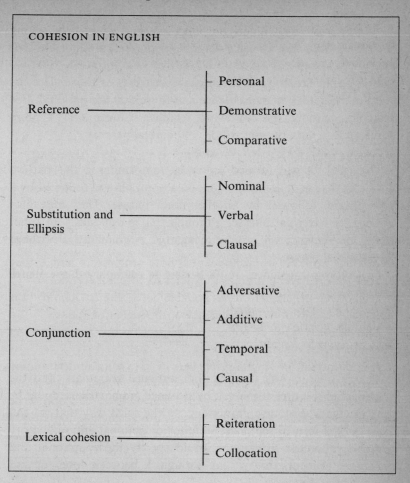

COHESION IN ENGLISH

Reference — Personal, Demonstrative, Comparative

Substitution and Ellipsis — Nominal, Verbal, Clausal

Conjunction — Adversative, Additive, Temporal, Causal

Lexical cohesion — Reiteration, Collocation

2.2.1   Units of analysis in discourse

Beyond the sentence

There are a number of different approaches to discourse analysis.
One is what I shall call the 'super sentence' school. This has

concerned itself with identifying and naming regularly recurring patterns in discourse. In some ways, this approach is similar to that taken by sentence grammarians whose aim is to formulate rules for describing the sentences of a language in terms of those elements that are obligatory to the sentence and those that are optional. For example, consider the following sentence pattern (NP = noun phrase; VP = verb phrase; AdvP = adverbial phrase):
Sentence = NP + VP + NP + [AdvP].

The 'rule' for well-formed sentences conforming to this pattern stipulates that sentences must contain a noun phrase, followed by a verb phrase, followed by another noun phrase. They may also contain an adverbial phrase, although this is optional – in other words, the sentence will still be recognized as grammatical without the adverbial phrase.

The following sentences could be said to exemplify this sentence pattern.
I enjoyed the movie yesterday.
She has an interview tomorrow.
They're seeing us tonight.
They might be joining us next week.

At one time, it was thought that sentence grammars, and the analytical procedures employed by sentence grammarians, could be used to create 'discourse grammars'. In the same way that we can describe well-formed sentences in terms of optional and obligatory elements, discourse grammars would specify those optional and obligatory elements that would distinguish between coherent and non-coherent discourse.

ACTIVITY

As you read the following extract from a second language classroom, see if you can identify any recurring patterns or regularities.

2f

T *The questions will be on different subjects, so, er, well, one will be about, er, well, 'some of the questions will be about politics, and some of them will be about, er, . . . what?*

S *History.*

T *History. Yes, politics and history and, um, and . . .?*

S *Grammar.*

T *Grammar's good, yes, . . . but the grammar questions were too easy.*

S *No.*

S *Yes, ha, like before.*

S *You can use . . . [inaudible]*

T *Why? The hardest grammar question I could think up – the hardest one, I wasn't even sure about the answer, and you got it.*

S *Yes.*

T *Really! I'm going to have to go to a professor and ask him to make questions for this class. Grammar questions that Azzam can't answer.*

[laughter]

Anyway, that's um, Thursday . . . yeah, Thursday. Ah, but today, er, we're going to do something different . . .

S *. . . yes . . .*

T *. . . today, er, we're going to do something where we, er, listen to a conversation – er, in fact, we're not going to listen to one conversation. How many conversation're we going to listen to?*

S *Three?*

(Nunan 1989)

This particular interaction seems to be made up of a series of recurring patterns. The teacher initiates the interaction, usually by asking a question to which he knows the answer, one or more of the students respond, and the teacher provides some sort of evaluation of the response.

INITIATION	T	*The questions will be on different subjects, so, er, well, one will be about, er, well, some of the questions will be about politics, and some of them will be about, er, . . . what?*
RESPONSE	S	*History.*
EVALUATION	T	*History. Yes, politics and history*
INITIATION	T	*and, um, and . . .?*
RESPONSE	S	*Grammar.*
EVALUATION	T	*Grammar's good, yes, . . .*

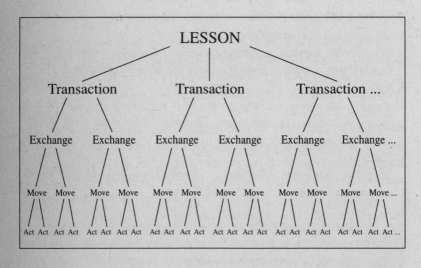

This pattern was first described by Sinclair and Coulthard (1975) who found that classroom interactions typically followed this fairly rigid pattern – regardless of the subject matter being taught or of the age range of the pupils in the class. Sinclair and Coulthard called the three-part structure an **exchange**. The three components making up the exchange they called **moves**, which were made up of **speech acts**. They found that entire lessons consisted of transactions, which were made up of these three-part exchanges. Each transaction within the lesson is explicitly signalled by a 'framing' move consisting of a phrase such as *OK, right, then, now*. Lessons could therefore be represented in the diagrammatic way shown opposite.

The basic building block of the lesson, then, is the speech act, which is an utterance described in terms of its function. Some of the speech acts identified by Sinclair and Coulthard are as follows:

ACT	FUNCTION	EXAMPLE
ACCEPT	Shows that the teacher has heard and accepts the student's utterance	*OK, Good*
BID	Signals student's desire to respond	*Sir! Teacher*
NOMINATION	Teacher selects student for response	*Azzam*

Sinclair and Coulthard used this model to draw up 'rules of discourse' which specified the optional and obligatory elements within a given exchange. Their method is therefore similar to that followed by sentence grammarians described earlier.

Sinclair and Coulthard were not necessarily interested in classrooms as interactional worlds in their own right. Their main aim was in developing a method for analysing discourse. Classrooms happened to be convenient places to start. In the first place, they are formal environments in which there are relatively clear rules of procedure. In addition, the roles, functions and power relationships between the participants are well defined.

ACTIVITY

Do you think that the model developed by Sinclair and Coulthard would be appropriate for analysing other types of interaction? Study the following conversation and develop a set of 'rules' for describing it.

2g
Tape: *Hold the line, please, all our operators are currently busy.* [music]
Operator: *Cabcharge – Account name?*

Customer: Macquarie University.
Operator: Passenger's name?
Customer: Nunan.
Operator: Pick-up address?
Customer: 13 Finch Avenue, East Ryde.
Operator: Is that a private house or flat?
Customer: Yes.
Operator: Going to?
Customer: The airport.
Operator: How many passengers?
Customer: One.
Operator: Are you ready now?
Customer: I'd like a cab for 2.30 pm, please.
Operator: We'll get a car to you as close to the time as we can.
Customer: Thank you.
(Nunan 1991)

ACTIVITY

How well does the rule fit the following interaction?

2h

Gary: . . . If I won the Lotto, I'd buy six or seven catamarans up at Noosa and sit them on the beach and hire them out and just rest there all the time.
Everyone (laughs)
Pauline: oh yes and then you – you'd want something to do
Garry: yes, you would but . . .
Bronwyn: mm no, look even if I'd won Lotto, I'd still have to come to work – I couldn't stand it
Garry: no, that's right
Bronwyn: I couldn't stand it
Pauline: yes, I think that um . . .
Pat: I'd buy my farm

Bronwyn: *I'd still – no, I need contact with people*
Pauline: *yes, that's right – I think I'd probably – if I'd paid off all my debts and wouldn't have that on my mind – I'd feel better – um but then I'd think I would like to work part time*
Bronwyn: *mm*
Gary: *mm*
Pauline: *you know, just for . . .*
Gary: *oh, I – I don't know*
Pauline: *being able to do things and then you'd still kind of . . .*
Gary: *I think I'd use the money a bit in investment*
(Economou 1986: 106)

You probably found that Sinclair and Coulthard's model was not particularly appropriate for analysing the telephone exchange between the Cabcharge operator and customer, but that you were able to develop a rule for describing this type of interaction, or at least identify the underlying question/answer pattern on which it appears to be based. In passing, it is worth noting that of the seven utterances designed to elicit answers in the piece of interaction, only three take the syntactic form of a question. This underlines the fact that there is no one-to-one relationship between form and function in discourse. You probably also found that the regularities apparent in 2g were different from those in 2 h.

It is possible to find other types of interaction in which the underlying patterns are relatively easy to perceive. Examples might include simple shopping transactions, parts of courtroom ritual, marriage ceremonies and so on. When it comes to casual conversation, it becomes much more difficult to devise rules for capturing the regularities in the interaction. This does not mean that there are no rules and regularities, merely that they are much more difficult to identify.

The problem in attempting to use the grammatical sentence as a metaphor for analysing discourse is that, like any metaphor, when applied too rigidly, it begins to break down. Let me illustrate this by returning to the sentence pattern I used at the beginning of this section. I suggested that sentences such as *I had a party yesterday* could be described in terms of a 'rule' – NP + VP + NP + [AdvP] – which specifies the optional and obligatory elements needed for the sentence to be considered well formed (that is, grammatical). Of course, we could take the analysis much further than this, specifying that the optional element may also occur at the beginning of the sentence as well as at the end, allowing sentences such as *Yesterday, I had a party.* We would also need to place restrictions on the NP and VP elements to make our rule more precise. For example, we would need to specify that the main verb in the VP must be transitive, thus disallowing sentences that do not require or allow an NP to follow the VP (for example, *Tom died. Annie smiled.*)

In the case of discourse, if we were to take this type of analysis beyond the level of the sentence, we would need to develop a 'discourse grammar' which would specify what utterances or sentences were optional and obligatory within a given discourse. This is, in a sense, what Sinclair and Coulthard (1975) attempted to do. However, tightly specifying what is or is not allowable beyond the level of the single utterance is almost impossible. Consider, for example, the following exchange in a French as a foreign language class:

2i
Students are brainstorming verbs for what they might do that evening . . .

> S: *What's 'run'?*
> MC: *'To run' . . . You run at night?*
> S: *Yeah. (MC writes 'courir' on the board.)*
> MC: *The past is 'couru'. What English word is related to 'courir', meaning 'to run'? What's running water?*
> 5 SS: *Flows?*
> MC: *In a river . . .*

S: Connecticut (*referring to the Connecticut River which separates Vermont from New Hampshire*).

SS: (*Laughter*) *No!*

10   MC: The running water in the middle of the river which is dangerous . . .

S: CURRENT

MC: The current, right?

SS: Very good. How'd you get that?

15   MC: How about a guy – usually a guy, sometimes a woman – who is a messenger? What's the word for . . .

SS: Court? Courier. COURIER.

MC: 'Courir' is 'to run' and 'couru' is the past.

(Freeman 1992: 67)

The researcher who observed and recorded this interaction comments:

[the teacher] controls the [vocabulary] activity to exercise her authority over the content. Questions or prompts, which require one-word responses from the students as a group, often generate guessing (see lines 5, 7, 12, 17). Through the exchange, a scaffold is built out of what the students know, to house the new material. The energy in such interactions is quite high; the whole group works together in a give-and-take with the teacher which is reminiscent of a tennis volley (see lines 4–5, 6–7, 10–12, 15–17). This varies the standard Inquiry–Response–Evaluation structure . . . found in most classroom discourse, concentrating instead on the exchange of Inquiry and Response. (Freeman 1992: 67)

We see here the difficulties that emerge when attempting to predict structural regularities in discourse. If we move beyond the classroom to less structured encounters such as parties or family birthdays, prediction becomes even more difficult.

Adjacency pairs

One response to the difficulty of identifying patterns in discourse has been to abandon the attempt to provide specifications for entire discourses, and instead to isolate regularly recurring patterns within the interaction. This has led to the identification of **adjacency pairs**, which are pairs of utterances that commonly co-occur. Examples of adjacency pairs include question–reply, introduction–greeting and so on. However, even here there are problems in predicting what will occur in discourse. Consider the following adjacency pair:

A: *How much was it?* – QUESTION
B: *Pound fifty.* – ANSWER

The interaction from which this adjacency pair was taken is actually considerably more complicated than a simple question–answer sequence. The transcript is set out below as text 2j.

2j
A: *How much was it?*
B: *Oh, you don't really want to know, do you?*
A: *Oh, tell me.*
A: *Wasn't cheap.*
A: *Was it a pound?*
B: *Pound fifty.*
(Author's data)

Here we see the adjacency pair separated by a number of intervening utterances which make up what is known as an **insertion sequence**. Such insertion sequences are common in all forms of interaction, and make the specification of optional and obligatory elements within discourse extremely difficult.

An additional problem with the 'super sentence' view of discourse is that it is unable to account for the interactional twists and turns that are always potentially likely to occur in all but the most formulaic of interactions. Consider the two classroom texts which follow. (In text 2l several individual students are interacting.)

2k
T   *What's the name of this? What's the name? Not in Chinese.*

Ss *Van. Van.*

T   *Van. What's in the back of the van?*

S   *Milk, milk.*

T   *Milk.*

Ss *Milk. Milk.*

T   *A milk van.*

S   *Milk van.*

T   *What's this man? . . . Driver.*

S   *Driver.*

(Nunan 1989)

21

S   *My mother is by bicycle. By bicycle, yes, many many water.*

T   *She had an accident?*

S   *China, my mother is a teacher, my father is a teacher. Oh, she go finish by bicycle, er, go to . . .*

S   *House?*

S   *No house, go to . . .*

S   *School?*

S   *My mother . . .*

T   *Mmm*

S   *. . . go to her mother.*

T   *Oh, your grandmother.*
    My grandmother. Oh, yes, by bicycle, by bicycle, oh is, em, accident. (Gestures)

T   *In water?*

S   *In water, yeah.*

T   *In a river!*

S   *River, yeah, river. Oh, yes, um, dead.*

Ss *Dead! Dead! Oh! (General consternation)*

T   *Dead? Your mother?*

(Nunan 1989)

Here we see two very different types of interaction occurring within several minutes of each other. The first is similar to the typical pattern of classroom interaction which we have already discussed. The second is much more like non-classroom interaction. The different pattern of interaction came about when the teacher stopped asking 'classroom display' questions – that is, questions to which she already knew the answer – and began asking genuine questions, sometimes referred to as 'referential' questions – that is, questions to which she did not know the answer. (We shall pursue this issue of the dynamics of interaction in the next chapter.)

2.3 'Given' and 'new' information

In English, there is a 'standard' word order of Subject + Verb + Object. In addition to the analysis of grammarians, there is some psycholinguistic evidence to suggest that second and foreign language learners acquire this standard word order before they acquire other sentence patterns (see, for example, Pienemann and Johnston 1987). The notion of a 'standard' word order, therefore has some sort of psycholinguistic as well as grammatical plausibility.

Let us consider a sentence often ascribed to the authors of phonics-based primers: *The cat ate the rat.* This sentence exhibits the standard Subject + Verb + Object structure. However, there are numerous other ways in which the semantic content of the sentence could be expressed. For example:

The rat was eaten by the cat.
It was the cat that ate the rat.
It was the rat that the cat ate.
What the cat did was ate the rat.
Ate the rat, the cat did.
The cat, it ate the rat.

Which of these options is actually selected by the writer or the speaker will depend on the context in which the utterance or sentence occurs and the status of the information within the discourse. One important consideration is whether the information has already been introduced into the discourse, or is assumed to be known to the reader or listener. Such information is referred to as **given information**. It contrasts with information which is introduced for the first time and which is known as **new information**. It is important to bear in mind, when considering the issue of given and new information in discourse, that it is the speaker/writer who decides what information should be considered given or new. As a rough rule of thumb, the new information in a sentence or utterance in English generally comes last. In the statement *The cat ate the rat*, the assumed knowledge is that the cat ate something and the new information is that it was a rat that got eaten.

We can see the close relationship between discourse considerations and grammatical structuring in relation to given and new information if we provide questions to which the above statements might be appropriate responses.

QUESTION: *What did the cat do?*
RESPONSE: *It ate the rat.* [*Or, The cat, it ate the rat.*]

QUESTION: *What happened to the rat?*
RESPONSE: *It was eaten by the cat.*

QUESTION: *Did the dog eat the rat?*
RESPONSE: *No, it was the cat that ate the rat.*

QUESTION: *Did the cat eat the mouse?*
RESPONSE: *No, it was the rat that was eaten by the cat.*

Notice that given information is referred to by pronouns when it occurs in context. In the first question–response pair above, the given information (that the cat did something) leads to the use of the pronoun *it* rather than the full noun phrase *the cat* in the response.

2.4   Theme and rheme

Another consideration in the arrangement of information in a sentence or utterance will be the prominence or importance that the speaker or writer wishes to give to different pieces of information. **Theme** is a formal grammatical category which refers to the initial element in a clause. It is the element around which the sentence is organized, and the one to which the writer wishes to give prominence. Everything that follows the theme is known as the **rheme**.

In the preceding section, we saw that the same information can be organized in different ways within the sentence. In the following sentences, the same information is presented:

The cat ate the rat.
The rat was eaten by the cat.

Thematically, however, both sentences are different. In the first sentence the theme is *The cat*. It is the cat and what the cat does that is of primary interest, and that forms the point of departure for the sentence. In the second sentence, it is the fate of the rat that is of primary interest.

Within the school of linguistics known as functional linguistics, three types of theme are identified – topical, interpersonal and textual. Topical themes have to do with the information conveyed in the discourse. In the above examples, the themes *the cat* and *the rat* are topical themes. Interpersonal themes, on the other hand, reveal something of the attitude of the speaker or reader. Finally, textual themes link a clause to the rest of the discourse. These different types of theme are illustrated in the sentences below which also show that a sentence can have more than one theme:

Frankly,	*the movie*	*was a waste of money.*
(INTERPERSONAL THEME)	(TOPICAL THEME)	

46

However,	*you*	*should see it and make up*
(TEXTUAL	(TOPICAL	*your own mind.*
THEME)	THEME)	

When moving beyond the sentence to discourse, the issue of **thematization** becomes particularly important as the writer has to arrange information in terms of given/new and also in terms of desired thematic prominence. The importance of theme/rheme structuring is illustrated in the following extracts. The first, from the opening chapter of *Peter Pan*, reads as its author J. M. Barrie had intended. In the second version, however, the thematic structure has been altered which gives a rather dislocated effect to the discourse.

2m

All children, except one strange little boy, grow up one day. Wendy knew she would have to grow up when she was just two years old. She was playing in the garden and picked a flower for her mother. Mrs Darling saw her daughter running towards her and smiled because Wendy looked so enchanting. 'Oh why can't you remain like this for ever!' she cried.
(J. M. Barrie *Peter Pan*)

2n

One day, all children, except one strange little boy, grow up. It was Wendy who knew she would have to grow up when she was only two years old. What happened was that she was in the garden playing, and a flower was picked by her for her mother. Enchanting, Wendy looked, and smiled, her mother did, because Wendy looked so enchanting running towards her. 'Remain like this forever, why can't you?' she cried.

In the altered version, the writer appears to be answering questions which have not been asked, and presupposing knowledge on the part of the readers which they cannot be expected to have.

ACTIVITY

Study sentence (a) below, and decide whether it should be followed by sentence (b) or sentence (c).

(a) *The victorious footballers stepped off the plane.*
(b) *Cheering fans immediately swamped them.*
(c) *They were immediately swamped by cheering fans.*

Which sentence would you prefer if the choice were between (d) or (e)

(d) *They were immediately buffeted by the wind.*
(e) *The wind immediately buffeted them.*

Finally, decide which you would select if the choice were between sentence (f) or sentence (g).

(f) *All the journalists were immediately smiled at by them.*
(g) *They immediately smiled at all the journalists.*

If the choice is between (b) or (c) as the continuation sentence, most people seem to prefer (c) because it maintains *the victorious footballers* as the theme of the emerging discourse. For the same reason, in the case of (d) and (e) the natural choice seems to be (d), and (g) is the preferred choice in the case of (f) and (g). (See Brown and Yule 1983a for a more detailed discussion on this point.)

2.5 Genre

The term 'genre' has been used for many years to refer to different styles of literary discourse such as sonnets, tragedies and romances. It highlights the fact that different types of discourse can be identified by their overall shape or generic structure. In recent times, the term has been adapted by functional linguists to refer to different types of communicative events (Martin 1984; Swales 1990). They argue that language exists to fulfil certain functions and that these functions will determine the overall shape or 'generic' structure of the discourse. This structure emerges as people communicate with one another – that is, it will have certain predictable stages. The communicative purpose will also be reflected in the basic building blocks of the discourse – that is, the words and grammatical structures themselves. In other words, different types of communicative events result in different types of discourse, and each of these will have its own distinctive characteristics. Some events result in sermons, others in political speeches, and yet others in casual conversations. While each sermon, political speech and casual conversation will be different, each discourse type will share certain characteristics which will set it apart from other discourse types.

ACTIVITY

Study the following texts. In what ways are they different? Can the differences be accounted for in terms of the functions of the texts?

2o
CURRIED FISH OR PRAWNS
  Chu-chi pla or goong
  9 large dried chillies (or to taste)
    chopped and soaked
  4 cloves of garlic
  6 shallots
  1 tablespoon diced lemongrass
  3 slices galanga
  1 teaspoon shrimp paste
  3 cups coconut cream
  3 tablespoons fish sauce
  1 tablespoon palm sugar

    1 cup shelled and deveined prawns,
      or a whole fish or fish slices
    Chilli strips and kaffir lime leaf
      shreds, for garnish

Blend or pound chilli, shallots, lemongrass, galanga, shrimp paste and ½ teaspoon salt to a paste. In a large heavy pan or wok, heat 1 cup coconut cream and fry until it has an oily surface, then add the paste and cook until thick and fragrant. Reduce further until oil seeps out from frying. Season to taste with fish sauce and sugar. Add remaining coconut cream and cook until thick and reduced. Add prawns or fish, stir lightly and simmer until just cooked. (Alternatively, the fish can be deep-fried in advance. The sauce is then poured over.) Garnish with chilli strips and lime leaf shreds and serve with cooked rice.

    Serves 3–4

(Based on an original recipe)

2p

A: *What did you do last night?*

B: *Well, Mum and Dad went out so we went to Marg's to sleep, and Sarah wouldn't go to sleep, and she wanted to ring Mum, and Marg said she couldn't, and so she cried, and so Marg combed her hair, and then she went to sleep. She was really naughty . . .*

A: *What time did she go to sleep?*

B: *Mmm – 'bout one o'clock.*

(Author's data)

2q

Hanging bungle uncovered

By GEOFF EASDOWN, MIKE EDMONDS and BARRY MacFADYN

MELBOURNE: A sensational development in the case of Ronald Ryan, the last man hanged in Australia, shows a bungle almost certainly cost him his life.

It was revealed last night that four letters written by jurors in the trial, appealing for Ryan not to be hanged, were never sent to the Victorian Cabinet which decided to execute him.

And a member of the Victorian Cabinet that voted 11–4 to hang Ryan, Sir Rupert Hamer, says the mercy pleas by four jury members could have saved Ryan.

(*The Advertiser,* 6 January 1992)

Each of these texts is very different in terms of its structure, grammar and physical appearance. Text 2o is a type of procedural text and has the following generic structure: *recipe*

— Title

— List of ingredients

— Procedure

Grammatically, the procedure consists of a set of instructions written in the imperative. Redundant items such as articles and prepositions are deleted, resulting in such characteristic phrases as: *pound chilli . . . heat 1 cup coconut cream . . . Add remaining coconut cream* etc.

The second extract, 2p, is taken from a conversation between a girl and her grandmother, and contains a **recount**. According to functional linguists, a recount consists of a sequence of events

51

which are initiated by an introduction and orientation, and which end with a comment and conclusion. We can see that, with the exception of a conclusion, this recount conforms to the proposed generic structure. Grammatically, recounts are characterized by the simple past tense, and the use of specific reference to people and places. We can see that this recount, in addition to its generic structure, also contains the grammatical items of simple past tense and specific reference.

INTRODUCTION	*Well, Mum and Dad went out*
ORIENTATION	*so we went to Marg's to sleep,*
EVENT	*and Sarah wouldn't go to sleep,*
EVENT	*and she wanted to ring Mum,*
EVENT	*and Marg said she couldn't,*
EVENT	*and so she cried,*
EVENT	*and so Marg combed her hair,*
EVENT	*and then she went to sleep.*
COMMENT	*She was really naughty.*

The third and final text, 2q, is an extract from a leading article in a newspaper. Its generic structure (at least the structure of the extract) is as follows:
— Title
— Author(s)
— Location
— Argument
— Supporting detail
— Supporting detail

Linguistically, the piece contains an agentless passive *It was revealed* ... It also contains emotively charged words such as *sensation, bungle, mercy, plea*. In terms of its layout and physical appearance, the text contains a large, eye-catching headline. The columns and assignment of each sentence to a separate paragraph are designed to make the piece easy to read.

These three texts illustrate some of the ways in which the overall structure, appearance and grammatical elements reflect the purposes for which the texts were created. The systematic relationship between language structure and function is described by Halliday in the following way:

Every text – that is, everything that is said or written – unfolds in some context of use; furthermore, it is the uses of language that, over tens of thousands of generations, have shaped the system. Language has evolved to satisfy human needs; and the way it is organised is functional with respect to those needs – it is not arbitrary. A functional grammar is essentially a 'natural' grammar, in the sense that everything in it can be explained, ultimately, by reference to how language is used. (Halliday 1985a: xiii)

2.5.1 Rhetorical patterns

Hoey (1983) argues that the ordering of information in discourse can reflect certain rhetorical relationships such as cause–consequence, problem–solution. He uses the following four sentences to illustrate the ways in which these relationships function in discourse.

2r
I opened fire.
I was on sentry duty.
I beat off the attack.
(*and*) *I saw the enemy approaching.*

These four sentences can be sequenced in twenty-four different ways. However, not all of these sequences will be acceptable as coherent discourse – for example, *I beat off the attack. I opened fire. I saw the enemy approaching. I was on sentry duty.* In fact, the twenty-four different versions could probably be graded on a continuum from completely unacceptable to completely acceptable. According to Hoey, only one sequence is completely acceptable: *I was on sentry duty. I saw the enemy approaching. I opened fire. I beat off the attack.*

ACTIVITY

Assuming that you agree with Hoey's assertion, what is it that makes this particular sequence acceptable? Can you think of any grammatical devices that might be employed to alter the sequencing of the information in the text?

Constraints on the ordering of information within a text are due in part to the relationships that exist between these elements. In text 2r there are two particular types of relationship: cause–consequence and instrument–achievement.

I was on sentry duty.
CAUSE → *I saw the enemy approaching.* → CONSEQUENCE → *I opened fire.*
INSTRUMENT → *I opened fire.* → ACHIEVEMENT → *I beat off the attack.*

There are in fact grammatical devices that can be employed to change the sequencing of the information in the text in acceptable ways. These include subordination (*While I was on sentry duty, I opened fire, because I saw the enemy approaching. I (thereby) beat off the attack.*) and conjunction (*I opened fire because I saw the enemy approaching when I was on sentry duty. By this means I beat off the attack.*)

2.6 Propositional analysis

In addition to the work undertaken within linguistics, there is a branch of cognitive psychology that investigates ways in which we produce and make sense of discourse. These psychologists are principally interested in how the human mind processes language, and how the structure and content of discourse affects what is processed and remembered. They are less interested in how language is used for communication than in the semantic structure of sentences and texts.

An important concept for these researchers is the **proposition**. A proposition is a single statement about some entity or event. A sentence may contain a single proposition or several propositions. A simple sentence such as *The cat ate the rat* contains a single proposition which would be represented as (*ATE, CAT, RAT*). Propositional analysis enables the researcher to compare texts that would not otherwise be comparable. Consider the following texts, which are approximately the same length, and which deal with a similar subject. Which, do you think, would be easier to read and recall?

2s

The bride was a plain woman in a big hat. She stood at the altar of St. Philip's, Church Hill, in Sydney a few days before Easter 1910 dressed for a voyage that would carry her across the world to Europe. She was thirty-two and this was a late and magnificent match for a woman on the threshold of spinsterhood. Great prospects lay before her, yet as Ruth swore to take her husband 'for better for worse, for richer for poorer' the crease of her mouth across that Withycombe jaw gave her the look of a woman who was faintly aggrieved. She carried that look for life.
(Marr 1991: 3)

2t

In Patrick White's world there are no accidents of birth. We are what we are born to be, free only to shape the life fate has given us. What we inherit can never be entirely denied. Escape is impossible. In middle age he once remarked expansively, 'I feel more and more, as far as creative writing is concerned, everything important happens to one before one is born.' He believed in blood and ancestors. He was delighted by the legend that a Withycombe was fool to Edward II.
(Marr 1991: 4)

Despite the fact that the texts are quite similar in their content and grammatical structures, it is difficult to say which text is easier to read and recall. Not only are language factors involved in the processing of discourse, but, as we shall see in the next chapter, the background knowledge and interests of the reader or listener have an important bearing on what is recalled. Psychologists have investigated the hypothesis that, all other things being equal (which they rarely are, outside of formal experiments), the difficulty of a text will be determined by the number of propositions it contains. In an experiment designed to test this hypothesis, Kintsch and Keenan (1973) had groups of subjects read two texts which were roughly the same length but which contained different numbers of propositions. (It is worth noting in passing that, while propositional analysis should enable researchers to experiment with 'natural' texts, the research of Kintsch, Keenan and others is based on artificially constructed texts, often of a highly contrived kind.)

In their study, Kintsch and Keenan predicted that sentence 1 would be more quickly read and understood than sentence 2.

2u

1. *Romulus, the legendary founder of Rome, took the women of the Sabine by force.*
2. *Cleopatra's downfall lay in her foolish trust in the fickle political figures of the Roman world.*

The propositional analysis of these two texts is as follows. While the sentences are approximately the same length, sentence 2 contains twice as many propositions. When Kintsch and Keenan carried out their experiment, they found that sentence 2 did indeed take significantly longer for subjects to comprehend.

PROPOSITIONAL ANALYSIS of SENTENCE 1

1 (*TOOK, ROMULUS, WOMEN, BY FORCE*)
2 (*FOUND, ROMULUS, ROME*)
3 (*LEGENDARY, ROMULUS*)
4 (*SABINE, WOMEN*)

PROPOSITIONAL ANALYSIS of SENTENCE 2

1 $(BECAUSE, A, B)$
2 $(FELL\ DOWN, CLEOPATRA) = A$
3 $(TRUST, CLEOPATRA, FIGURES) = B$
4 $(FOOLISH, TRUST)$
5 $(FICKLE, FIGURES)$
6 $(POLITICAL, FIGURES)$
7 $(PART\ OF, FIGURES, WORLD)$
8 $(ROMAN, WORLD)$

In addition to the discovery that the number of propositions in a text will have an important bearing on how easily a reader or listener will understand it, researchers have also found that there is a hierarchical relationship among the propositions in a text. In other words, the propositions are not all equally important. Subsequent research has shown that the more central a proposition is to the argument of the writer, the more likely it is to be recalled by a reader.

PROJECT

Select a written text or text extract. This may be either a fictional or factual text. Analyse the text according to the following:
— cohesion
— information structuring (theme / rheme; given / new structures)
— overall patterns or generic structure.

SUMMARY

- Coherent discourse contains certain identifiable structural devices and characteristics which distinguish it from random sentences or utterances.
- Cohesion consists of certain linguistic devices, including pronouns and conjunctions, which enable the writer or speaker to make relationships between entities and events explicit.

- Certain kinds of discourse can be distinguished from other kinds of discourse in terms of their distinctive, recurring patterns. For example, classroom discourse and courtroom discourse both contain questions and answers. However, the ways in which these combine in context will differ.
- The position of information within the sentences in a text will indicate whether it is given or new information. If the information is poorly arranged, then the text can be difficult to follow.
- The arrangement of information within the sentences or utterances in a text will also reflect the emphasis and focus of the writer or speaker.
- The communicative purposes for which a text is created will be reflected in its overall structure (what I have called generic structure), and also in the grammatical features it contains. Compare, for example, recipes and advertisements or narratives and descriptions.

3 Making sense of discourse

3.1 Discourse coherence

In the preceding chapter we looked at some of the building blocks of discourse. The focus of attention was therefore firmly on the text itself. In this chapter, we shall bring the users into the picture. In other words, we shall look in greater detail at speakers and listeners, readers and writers, as they construct and interpret discourse.

At the beginning of chapter 2, we examined some of the linguistic characteristics of coherent discourse. We saw that coherent discourse was distinguished from random sentences by the existence of certain text-forming, cohesive devices. In this section I wish to look in greater detail at the role of cohesion in the establishment of coherent discourse.

ACTIVITY

Study the following texts and decide which are coherent and which are random sentences. In the process, try and identify the basis for your decisions.

3a
A: *That's the telephone.*
B: *I'm in the bath.*
A: *OK.*
(Widdowson 1978)

3b

A: *What's this?*
B: *That? It's a watch. Why?*
A: *Funny looking one if you ask me.*
(Author's data)

3c

Charles Dickens was born on the seventh of February 1812, the year of victory and the year of hardship. He came crying into the world in a small first-floor bedroom in an area known as New Town or Mile End, just on the outskirts of Portsmouth where his father, John Dickens, worked in the Naval Pay Office. His mother, Elizabeth, is reported to have claimed that she went to a ball on the night before his birth . . .
(Ackroyd 1990: 1)

3d

A: *How much was it?*
B: *Oh, you don't really want to know, do you?*
A: *Oh, tell me.*
B: *Wasn't cheap.*
A: *Was it a pound?*
B: *Pound fifty.*
(Author's data)

3e

Psycholinguistic reading skills are not invariant. Reading skills are something that English teachers work hard to develop. Singapore's economy has developed rapidly in recent years. We shall need to economise if we are to save money.

Most readers agree that the only random collection of sentences is text 3e. All of the other passages are seen as being coherent. Yet these passages do not seem to conform to the principle established in chapter 2 – namely, that coherent texts are distinguished from random sentences by the existence of text-forming, cohesive devices.

The utterances in text 3a seem to go together despite the fact that there is no evidence of cohesion. In text 3e, on the other hand, each sentence shares a link with the one which precedes it; despite this, there is general agreement that the sentences do not belong together. Clearly, cohesion is neither necessary nor sufficient for the creation of coherent discourse. How can we explain coherence in the case of texts 3a, 3b, 3c and 3d, and the lack of connectivity in the case of text 3e?

It would seem that in the case of the first four texts it is possible to construct a context in which these pieces of language could conceivably have taken place. This is not the case with text 3e, although I should point out that with a little ingenuity it is probably possible to construct a context for any two of the four sentences. For example, consider the two sentences: *Reading skills are something that English teachers work hard to develop. Singapore's economy has developed rapidly in recent years.* As they stand, these sentences do not seem to relate to each other. However, when an extended context is provided, they are readily seen as coherent.

3f

A: *Education, particularly literacy, is extremely important for developing the full potential of a society.*

B: *True. Take our situation here in Singapore. Reading skills are something that English teachers work hard to develop.*

A: *Singapore's economy has developed rapidly in recent years. Would you say that this has been due, at least in part, to the educational system?*

B: *I certainly would!*

Text 3a has been taken from Widdowson (1978), who uses it to support his argument that cohesion is neither necessary nor sufficient for the establishment of coherence. He goes on to suggest that we are able to recognize this text as coherent by creating a context and then identifying the functions that each utterance fulfils within that context. Most native speakers would create a domestic situational context in which the following functions are assigned to each utterance:

UTTERANCE	FUNCTION
A: That's the telephone.	REQUEST
B: I'm in the bath.	EXCUSE
A: OK.	ACCEPTANCE OF EXCUSES

In creating a meaningful context and identifying the functions of each utterance, coherence is established. As a result, the missing bits of conversation, which would make it cohesive as well as coherent, could be restored. Such a cohesive conversation might run as follows:

A: That's the telephone. Can you answer it, please?
B: No, I'm sorry, I can't answer it because I'm in the bath.
A: OK, I'll answer it then.

Of course, the interlocutor can always deliberately misinterpret the functional intention of the speaker for humorous, ironic or other effects, as the following example shows.

3g
(*A is addressing her husband who is clearing out a garden shed.*)
A: Are you wearing gloves?
B: No.
A: What about the spiders?
B: They're not wearing gloves either.
(Author's data)

Although there is no surface cohesion between A's two utterances, *Are you wearing gloves?* and *What about the spiders?*, B readily perceives that they are coherent in at least two ways:
1. *What about the spiders? You might get bitten, if you don't wear gloves.*
2. *What about the spiders, are they wearing gloves?*

If the subject of the second utterance happened to be human, the second interpretation would be the preferred one (for example, if the wife had said, *What about the children?*). Here it would be quite natural for the clause *are they wearing gloves?* to be omitted. However, given the non-human subject of the wife's second utterance, the second interpretation is highly improbable. We shall charitably assume that the husband chooses the second interpretation for humorous effect. If the subject of the second utterance had been inanimate – for example, *What about the nails?* – then the second interpretation would be merely silly.

Edmonson (1981) also explores the issue of what distinguishes text from non-text (that is, coherent from non-coherent texts). He claims that it is difficult to create non-texts from random sentences because some sort of context can generally be created which will give coherence to any set of sentences. He challenges van Dijk's (1977) assertion that the following two sentences are incoherent:

3h
We will have guests for lunch.
Calderon was a great writer.

Edmonson argues that any native speaker will immediately see a causal link between these two sentences. (Before reading further, see whether you can construct a context which might lend coherence to these two sentences.)

Edmonson provides the following context:

3i
Did you know Calderon died exactly one hundred years ago today? Good heavens! I'd forgotten. The occasion shall not pass unnoticed. We will have guests for lunch. Calderon was a great Spanish writer. I shall invite Professor Wilson and Señor Castellano right away . . .
(Edmonson 1981: 13)

Two points which should be noted here are, firstly, that in order to provide interpretable texts that lack cohesive markers, Widdowson and Edmonson provide very brief examples – three utterances in the case of the first, and two sentences in the case of the second. One wonders how far either text could be extended without the appearance of a cohesive device. The second point with which one might want to take issue is Edmonson's claim that any native speaker will immediately be able to establish the coherence of van Dijk's two sentences. In fact, the provision of an appropriate context requires a reasonable level of ingenuity.

Despite these quibbles, I am in basic agreement with the notion that cohesion does not 'create' coherence, for reasons that I shall outline in greater detail later. However, I believe that Widdowson and Edmonson overstate their case. Their argument assumes that each utterance has a clearly identifiable function, the perception of which is somehow independent of the ideas or propositions expressed. In Widdowson's example, it is claimed that coherence is achieved through perception of the functions being performed by each utterance. This enables the complete propositional content of each utterance to be supplied by the listener. However, the issue of which comes first – perception of the full **propositional meaning**, or the function performed by each utterance – is a 'chicken and egg' argument. In this particular instance, I believe that perception of the propositions must either precede or occur simultaneously with the recognition of functions. Thus, for interlocutor B in Widdowson's example to recognize that *That's the telephone* is functioning as 'request', he or she must also have perceived the unstated proposition *Could you answer it, please?* Someone trying to comprehend spoken or written discourse must simultaneously perceive both the propositional meaning and functional intention of the speaker or writer.

I believe that interpreting discourse, and thus establishing coherence, is a matter of readers/listeners using their linguistic knowledge to relate the discourse world to people, objects, events and states of affairs beyond the text itself. While any piece of language is ultimately interpretable with reference to extra-linguistic context, it is going too far to conclude that the language itself is somehow irrelevant or unnecessary.

3.2   Speech acts

In the preceding section, we saw that explicit, cohesive links between utterances were insufficient to account for the coherence of
discourse, and that such coherence depends on the ability of the
language users to recognize the functional role being played by
different utterances within the discourse. In the next section, we
shall look at the role of background knowledge in the interpretation of discourse. Before turning to the role of background knowledge, however, I should like to explore the issue of language
functions, or speech acts, a little further. Speech acts are simply
things people do through language – for example, apologizing,
complaining, instructing, agreeing and warning. The term 'speech
act' was coined by the linguistic philosopher Austin (1962) and
developed by another philosopher Searle (1969). They maintained
that, when using language, we not only make propositional statements about objects, entities, states of affairs and so on, but we
also fulfil functions such as requesting, denying, introducing, apologizing etc. Identifying the speech act being performed by a particular utterance can only be done if we know the context in which the
utterance takes place. The functional intention of the speaker is
known as the **illocutionary force** of the utterance.

ACTIVITY

Consider the following utterance: *There's a Rhodesian ridgeback in
the garden*. How many different functions can you identify for this
utterance? Create a context for each of these.

EXAMPLE: WARNING

Context: A: *There's no answer at the front door. Shall I try the
back?*

B: *I shouldn't, if I were you. There's a Rhodesian ridgeback in the garden.*

During the 1970s, some language specialists began to argue that teaching learners the formal elements of second and foreign languages was insufficient, and that, following the work of people such as Austin and Searle, teachers should also teach language functions. Accordingly, teaching materials and procedures began to reflect this change of emphasis.

ACTIVITY

Study the following conversations, and identify the functions they are attempting to teach.

3j

Liz: Do you like jazz, Tom?
Tom: No, I don't like it very much. Do you?
Liz: It's OK. What kind of music do you like?
Tom: Well, I like rock a lot.
Liz: U2. How about you? Do you like them?
Tom: No, I don't. I can't stand them.
(Richards et al. 1990: 23)

3k

Dave: There's a jazz concert at the Blue Note on Friday. Would you like to go?
Joan: Yeah, that sounds good! What time is the concert?
Dave: It's at 10 o'clock.
Joan: Great! Let's go.
(Richards et al. 1990: 25)

3l

Carolyn: Excuse me – are you Mrs. Baxter?
Mrs. Baxter: Yes, I am.
Carolyn: I'm Carolyn Duval.
Mrs. Baxter: Nice to meet you, Ms. Duval.
(Warshawsky 1992: A2)

3m

A: (*Dials number*) *Rrring, rrring.*
B: *Directory Assistance.*
A: *I'd like the number of Jane Schaefer.*
B: *Could you spell the last name, please?*
A: *S-C-H-A-E-F-E-R*
B: *The number is 555-5275.*
A: *Thank you.*
B: *You're welcome.*
(Warshawsky 1992: A17)

3.3   Background knowledge

The things we know about the world assist us in the interpretation of discourse.

ACTIVITY

The inadequacy of linguistic knowledge (that is, knowledge of the vocabulary, grammar and discourse features) alone for interpreting discourse is readily demonstrated. Read the following passage through quickly and then put the book aside and write down as much of the story as you can recall.

3n

If the balloons popped, the sound wouldn't be able to carry since everything would be too far away from the correct floor. A closed window would prevent the sound from carrying, since most buildings tend to be well insulated. Since the whole operation depends on a steady flow of electricity, a break in the middle of the wire would also cause problems. Of course, the fellow could shout, but the human voice is not loud enough to carry that far. An additional problem is that a wire could break on the instrument. Then there could be no accompaniment to the message. It is clear that the best situation would involve less distance. Then there would be fewer potential problems. With face-to-face contact, the least number of things could go wrong.

Most native speakers have no trouble comprehending the grammatical structures and vocabulary items in this story. Despite this, they have a great deal of trouble understanding what the text is all about, and even greater difficulty in providing an oral or written summary.

The passage is from a well-known study by Bransford and Johnson (1972) which demonstrated the importance of context and background information for the interpretation of discourse. They found that subjects who were asked to listen to the text and recall it had a great deal of difficulty. However, another group of subjects who were provided with a picture were able to recall virtually all of the text. This picture showed a man serenading his girlfriend. The girl was leaning out of the window of an apartment, and the sound was carried to her through some speakers which were suspended by a bunch of balloons.

This interaction between the world of the text and the world outside the text is exploited by writers in many different ways. For example, some writers often create humorous or satirical effects by juxtaposing the real and imaginary worlds. The following text illustrates this process. To someone unfamiliar with events in the former Soviet Union, the text would make as little sense as the 'serenade' text above.

3o

The former Comrade Chairman of the former Communist Party, former president of the former empire and former photo opportunity, slogged up the last six flights of stairs to his office. The stairs were well worn, particularly in the centre of each step where two deep grooves commemorated the heel-marks of generations of politically incorrect thinkers who had been dragged to the basement by men

with no necks. Later, they had been released as politically correct
mulch. Somewhere in the basement was a room full of their hats,
sorted and labelled. The former Comrade Chairman wondered what
had happened to them. The former re-education staff had probably
opened a shop, he decided. There wasn't much call for trained
interrogators who could correct political error while forcing the
miscreants' kneecaps down their throats, outside the more progressive
Western universities. He hoped the shop was doing well. Everyone
needed a hat, if only to gather up stray potatoes down at the shunting
yards, and it was just the kind of entrepreneurial spirit he knew
lurked beneath the coarse woollen exterior of the former Soviet
people, even the horrible ones.
(Cook 1991: 194)

3.3.1   Using background knowledge: propositional level

With the insight that there is more to comprehending discourse
than knowing the words on the page, have come attempts to
provide theoretical models that can explain the ways in which our
knowledge of the world guides our efforts to comprehend discourse.
Much of this work has been carried out by researchers in the field
of artificial intelligence. Their aim is to develop programs that
will enable computers to comprehend and produce natural
discourse.

Frame theory

One well-known theory is **frame theory**. This suggests that human
memory consists of sets of stereotypical situations, or 'frames',
which are constructed out of our past experiences. These provide a
framework which we use to make sense of new experiences. For
example, our former experiences of 'going to the doctor' provide us
with a frame that enables us to predict what is likely to occur when

we next visit the doctor. Of course, our expectations are not always fulfilled, and, when this happens, we must modify our pre-existing frames to accommodate the experiences.

While this theory might appeal to our common-sense notions about how comprehension works, it does have a number of problems. One major problem is that it provides no explanation of why one frame might be selected rather than another.

ACTIVITY

Read the following text and decide which 'frame' should be used to guide comprehension.

3p
Recession or no recession, retailers were preparing yesterday for the expected onslaught of thousands of bargain hunters. Shops around the country were getting ready to open their doors for the first day of traditional after-Christmas clearance sales, with one large retail chain already predicting record trading levels.
(*The Australian*, Friday 27 December 1991)

Does this text conjure up a 'recession' frame, a 'Christmas' frame, an 'economy' frame, a 'shopping' frame, or some other frame? It is not immediately apparent which of these frames should be invoked, and frame theory gives little insight into the mental processes which guide the selection of one frame rather than another. Of course, the more text one has, the greater the chance of selecting the appropriate frame, and often, as listener or reader, we have to reserve judgement for some time until we have enough information to make a choice. Writers sometimes gain dramatic, ironic or humorous effect by producing texts that are deliberately ambiguous, and, in some cases, by deliberately leading readers up the garden path, encouraging them to invoke the wrong frame.

Schema theory

The term 'schema' was coined as long ago as 1932 by the psychologist Bartlett in his classic study of how human memory works. Like frame theory, **schema theory** suggests that the knowledge we carry around in our heads is organized into interrelated patterns. These are constructed from all our previous experiences and they enable us to make predictions about future experience. Given the fact that making sense of discourse is a process of using both our linguistic knowledge and also our content knowledge, these schemata or 'mental film scripts' are extremely important.

The central insight provided by researchers using mental models such as frame and schema theory is that meaning does not come neatly prepackaged in aural and written texts. Widdowson (1978) has suggested that texts are little more than elaborate 'signposts' to the speaker or writer's original meanings, and that the reader or listener must use his or her linguistic and content knowledge to reconstruct the original meanings of the creator of the discourse.

In a later work, Widdowson (1983) provides a novel reinterpretation of schema theory from the perspective of discourse comprehension. He argues that there are two dimensions or levels to any given discourse – a systemic level and a schematic level. The systemic level includes the reader or listener's linguistic knowledge, while the schematic level relates to background content knowledge. In making sense of a given piece of discourse, we try and match up our own schematic knowledge with that of the writer or speaker. In doing so, we have to interpret what we read or hear. (Cicourel (1973) was one of the first researchers to point out the importance of interpretation to comprehension. He showed that we use procedures of interpretation to supply meanings that do not actually appear in the discourse itself.)

Widdowson (1983) has shown how these interpretive procedures might work in making sense of discourse. He argues that a major task for someone listening to or reading a piece of discourse is to keep track of the various things and events that are referred to within the discourse. In doing so, he or she can make use of the various cohesive devices we looked at in chapter 2. It is often assumed that the ability to track cohesive relationships through a text is a fairly straightforward business. Consider the following text:

I saw John yesterday. He gave me his hat.

Most people would assume that the hat belongs to John. However, Widdowson demonstrates that the ability to establish and track such relationships often involves more than simple identification. There are cases where we need to interpret what we see or hear. Widdowson illustrates this point through a number of rather bizzare texts, the first of which is as follows. As you read it, consider what the underlined reference items refer to.

3q

Statistical probability was discovered in a teapot. A postman saw <u>it</u> <u>there</u> and connected in to a petrol pump. <u>He</u> was wearing silk pyjamas at the time. They were old and dusty.

As Widdowson rightly points out, while the reader might be surprised by this surrealistic piece of prose, there is no difficulty in identifying *it* with *statistical probability*, *he* with *postman*, and *there* with *teapot*. Other cases are more difficult. What, for instance, does *it* refer to in the following text?

3r

Statistical probability was discovered in a teapot. A postman saw <u>it</u> and connected <u>it</u> to a petrol pump. <u>It</u> was old and dusty.

Determining what *it* refers to now becomes more difficult as there are two possible antecedents for the first *it* (*statistical probability* and *a teapot*) and three for the second (*statistical probability* and *a teapot* and *a petrol pump*). Since we cannot use our background knowledge to help us, we are unable to say what *it* refers to.

Consider now a third text.

3s

Statistical probability was discovered in a teapot. A postman rinsed it out. He had no idea what it was of course.

In this text we can appeal to our knowledge of the world to determine what *it* refers to. We know that teapots are occasionally rinsed out, and therefore assume that the first *it* refers to *teapot*. As we also assume that postmen are familiar with teapots, we would assign the second *it* to *statistical probability*. The point of all this is that in many cases discourse processing depends, not only on the identification of cohesive relationships, but also on our knowledge of the world.

We engage in these interpretive procedures more frequently than might be imagined. Consider the following textual fragment from a popular magazine.

3t

I believe all children have a mystical empathy with nature. We come into this world 'trailing clouds of glory' as the poet Wordsworth put it.
(Clyne 1991)

Here, there are no direct links between the first sentence and the second, and so we need to use our background knowledge to create the links and establish a relationship between the metaphorical phrase *clouds of glory* and the *mystical empathy* that children are claimed to have with nature. Most native speakers have little difficulty in identifying the relationship.

3.3.2 Using background knowledge: functional level

Let us now look at how background knowledge might help us interpret discourse on a functional level. When studying functions, the question is not 'what is the speaker/writer trying to tell us about events and things in the world?' but 'what is the speaker/

writer trying to achieve through language?' Once again, Widdowson (1983) provides a lively piece of (fictional) interaction to demonstrate the points he wishes to make.

3u

A: *I have two tickets to the theatre tonight.*
B: *My examination is tomorrow.*
A: *Pity.*

What are our fictional speakers trying to do here? According to Widdowson, there are implicit assumptions on both sides that A's first statement is an invitation. B's response, which, on the surface, has little to do with A's statement, is taken as a refusal of the invitation. This is recognized in A's final remark. Of course, the encounter may not have gone quite as smoothly as this. Consider the following exchange, in which A's opening gambit is intended as an invitation. What do you think the speakers are trying to do in the other utterances in the exchange?

A: *I have two tickets for the theatre tonight.*
B: *Good for you. What are you going to see?*
A: *Measure for Measure.*
B: *Interesting play. Hope you enjoy it.*

The negotiation is not going to plan, and A has to renegotiate to return to his original discourse strategy.

A: *Look, are you free tonight?*
B: *I'm not sure, why?*

The message is still not getting across, so he tries again.

A: *Well, I'd like to invite you to come to the theatre with me.*
B: *Well, actually my examination is tomorrow.*

Now Widdowson allows A to be obtuse.

A: *I know, so is mine. What's that got to do with it?*
(Widdowson 1983: 44–5)

Notice how these negotiating procedures depend crucially on the participants knowing what each utterance stands for functionally (that is, 'invitation', 'polite refusal' etc.).

ACTIVITY

Study the following text and answer these questions. As you do the task, make a mental note of the strategies you use to make sense of the text.
— How many words can you make out?
— What type of text do you think it is?
— What do you think the text is about?
— What do you think is the purpose of the text?
— What language is the text written in?

3v

TOK BILOG GAVMAN

  Sipos yu painim sompela Japan i les long pait, yu gifim dispela pas. Sipos i savi wakabaut, i kan kam ontaim yupela nau painim soldia bilong yumi. Im i sik tumas, orait, yu brinim tok.

  Tok im gut, mipela nokan kilim ol, kalabus dasol, nau salim ol iko long Astralia, na weitim pait i pinis.
WOK BILOG GAVMAN. I GAT PEI.

ACTIVITY

The text is written in New Guinean Tok Pisin. The following extract is a conversation between two individuals who attempted to decode the Tok Pisin text. In the extract they are discussing the strategies they used to make sense of the decontextualized text. Make a list of these strategies. What are the similarities and differences between their strategies and the one which you used? How reasonable do you find their interpretation?

3w

A: I . . . think one of the strategies is that is that . . . I feel I know a little bit of the language and I'm trying to draw on anything I've seen before or heard before that I can relate back to . . .

B: *We're also using what we know about English and relating the words to English. But as well as that you start trying to decipher the actual grammar of the language, so things like (pronouns and) 'sompela', 'yupela' and the other one which I've lost at the moment – 'mipela' – presumably have something to do with with umm (but also) the way in which the grammar is organised, like 'som' and 'yu' and 'mi mifela', 'yufela' and whatever.*

A: *But also, what we've done so far is try to decipher it more or less word by word, and we're only just beginning to get a sense of the context or the background knowledge or or the kind of the discourse as a whole so um – it's interesting that we've started by trying to do it word-by-word . . .*

B: *Although we also get to bits that we can't do and leave it and then go on . . .*

A: *And then come back . . .*

B: *. . . when you've got a better sense of what comes after to try and actually . . . almost like a cloze test where you try to . . . to reconstruct what ought to go where on the basis of having read on.*

A: *I'm trying to think of what kind of connections there are between Australia and Japan and . . . in Papua New Guinea the kind of connections between Australia and Japan would be the war really, wouldn't they?*

B: *Either that or investment – mining.*

A: *Yes, oh, that's true – could be investment, yeah.*

B: *So, it could be there's someone who's done this work and hasn't got paid.*

A: *Or it could be that they don't feel that investment with and contact with Australia have been very profitable and they're now turning to to Japan for investment opportunities with other countries.*

ACTIVITY

Most people can decipher a few words, but have a great deal of difficulty in deciding the text type and purpose. However, given a context for the text, they can make much more sense of it. The next paragraph provides a context. After you have read it, consider again the five questions above. Does the context enable you to make more sense of the text?

The original text is printed on a piece of paper which is accompanied by two illustrations. The first of these shows a New Guinea highlander in a jungle setting peering around a tree at a wounded Japanese soldier who is holding up a piece of paper. The second illustration shows the highlander, the piece of paper in his hand, leading three Australian soldiers, one of whom carries a first aid kit, through the jungle. On the reverse of the paper is a message in Japanese.

Given the context, most readers can identify the text as part of a leaflet designed by the Australian army and used in New Guinea during the Second World War. It was intended that the leaflet should be used by wounded Japanese soldiers to give to natives, who would lead Australian soldiers to the wounded Japanese soldier. Here is the translation of the message, written in Tok Pisin, and the Japanese text.

TOK PISIN LITERAL TRANSLATION
GOVERNMENT'S MESSAGE
If you find some Japanese who refuse to fight, you give them this letter. If he is able to walk and come on time, you (plural) must look for our soldier. If he is very sick, OK, you bring the message.
Tell them clearly that we cannot kill them, but (we will) take them as prisoner only and send them to Australia, and (they will) wait for the war to end.
GOVERNMENT'S WORK (JOB)
HAS A WAGE (REWARD)
(Translated by Philip Aratiso.)

JAPANESE TRANSLATION

You must have done everything you could do. This must be your present situation and true feeling. It will be totally pointless if you terminate your lives at this stage. Leave where you are and come to us. We already have thousands of soldiers from the Japanese military who were in a similar situation to you. They voluntarily came here and have chosen to serve post-war Japan. In other words, each of them has chosen not to die in vain, but to survive, and to work for the post-war Japanese nation. It goes without saying, of course, that we have facilities such as medical treatment, studying and moral training. The English letter on the back is to instruct the local residents to guide you to us. You will be transferred immediately from the war zone to Australia's camps, hospitals, etc.

(Translated by Tomoko Koyama.)

In this section, we have looked at the contributions of the listener and reader in interpreting discourse. In the next section, we shall build on this discussion when we look at two competing models of the way we make sense of discourse.

3.4　How we process discourse

Over the years, there has been considerable controversy over the mental processes used by readers and listeners as they interpret discourse and relate it to their background knowledge and experience. Particularly controversial has been the debate over **bottom-up** and **top-down** models of how the comprehension process works.

3.4.1　Bottom-up processing

In bottom-up processing, the smallest units of language are identified first, and these are 'chained together' to form the next highest unit; these units in turn are then chained together to form the next highest unit and so on. In the case of reading, the bottom-up model assumes that the reader first identifies each letter in a text as it is encountered. These letters are blended together and mentally 'sounded out' to enable the reader to identify the words that they make up; words are chained together to form sentences; sentences are linked together into paragraphs; and paragraphs are tied together to form complete texts. Comprehension is thus the final step in a lengthy process of decoding ever larger units of language.

Until comparatively recently, the bottom-up approach dominated reading research and theory. It is the basis of the vast majority of reading schemes, and also of phonics-based reading primers. Although there is now a great deal of empirical evidence that demonstrates the inadequacy of this bottom-up model, it still has many adherents within the language teaching profession.

One reason for the survival of this model (particularly in the initial teaching of reading) in the face of empirical attack is that it seems a reasonable and logical explanation of what happens when we read. Letters do represent sounds, and, despite the fact that, in English, twenty-six written symbols have to represent over forty aural symbols, there is a degree of consistency. On the surface it seems more logical to teach beginning readers to exploit the systematic correspondences between written and spoken symbols than to teach them to recognize the words they encounter by memorizing each word's unique shape.

One of the assumptions underlying phonics is that once a reader has blended the sounds together to form a word, that word will then be recognized. Implicit in the approach is the assumption that the reader possesses an oral vocabulary that is extensive enough to allow decoding to proceed. Such an assumption is questionable with both first and second language readers. Most primary and elementary teachers are familiar with children who can decode written symbols into their aural equivalent and 'sound out' words, and who therefore appear able to read, but who do not actually understand what they read.

A number of other major criticisms have been made of the bottom-up approach to reading, much of it based on research into human memory. The first of these criticisms is that, in English at least, with twenty-six symbols and over forty sounds, the correspondences between letters and sounds are both complex and relatively unpredictable. It was acknowledgement of this complexity and unpredictability that led to the development of initial reading primers, composed almost entirely of words with regular sound-symbol correspondences. Although this made word recognition easier, it led to stories that were unnatural and tedious for children to read.

Another criticism, once again growing out of research into human memory, is that the processing of each letter as it is encountered in a text would slow reading down to the point where it would be difficult for meaning to be retained. For example, it takes a quarter to a third of a second to recognize and assign the appropriate sound to a given letter of the alphabet. At this rate, given the average length of English words, readers would only be able to read around sixty words a minute. In fact, it has been demonstrated that the average reader can read and comprehend 250–350 words a minute. Given the fact that we can only hold in working memory about seven different items at any one time, the reader should, according to the bottom-up model, very often forget the beginning of a sentence (and often a word) before reaching the end.

In addition, it is often impossible to decode letters and words in a serial manner (that is, decode each letter or word as it is encountered). There are times when it is impossible to make decisions about how letters ought to sound until one actually knows the word in which the letter appears. Similarly, there are times when it is impossible to decide how a word ought to sound, until one knows the meaning of the clause or sentence in which it appears. If, for example, in reading a passage, one encountered the sequence of letters *ho* —, it would be impossible to say what sound the *o* represented until one knew whether the context was *house*, *horse*, *hot*, *hoot* etc. In the same way, it is impossible to say how the word *read* ought to sound until one knows whether the sentence containing the word is written in the present or the past tense.

Evidence against the bottom-up approach has also come from investigations of errors made when reading a text aloud. Fluent readers do not always read the words that are on the page. Deviations from the text (called 'miscues') provide evidence that something other than mechanical decoding is going on when readers process written discourse.

3.4.2 Top-down processing

Evidence from sources such as the reading miscues have led to an alternative model of language processing known as the top-down approach. This operates in the opposite direction from bottom-up processing: listeners/readers make sense of discourse by moving from the highest units of analysis to the lowest.

Cambourne (1979) provides the following diagrammatic representation of the way top-down processing works in relation to reading.

```
┌─────────────────────────────────────────────────────────────┐
│                                                               │
│  TOP-DOWN PROCESSING MODEL                                    │
│                                                               │
│  Past experience  → Selective  → Meaning  → Sound            │
│  and language       aspects                 pronunciation    │
│  intuitions         of print                if necessary     │
│                                                               │
└─────────────────────────────────────────────────────────────┘
```

According to this theory, the listener/reader makes use of his or her background knowledge of the subject at hand, knowledge of the overall structure of the text, knowledge and expectations of how language works, and motivation, interests and attitudes towards the text and the context it contains. Rather than decoding every symbol, or even every word, he or she forms hypotheses about what might follow in the text and then reviews or 'samples' these to determine whether the original hypotheses were correct.

Top-down strategies that good readers employ, and that can be taught to young readers, include the following:

1. Using background knowledge to assist in comprehending a particular text;

2. Scanning the text for headings, sub-headings and non-text material such as pictures, graphs and diagrams to acquire a broad understanding before more detailed reading;

3. Skimming the text and thinking about the content, and then writing down a number of questions that you would like the text to answer for you;

4. Identifying the genre of the text (knowing that you are about to read a procedural, instructive, allegorical text etc. can facilitate reading comprehension);

5. Discriminating between more and less important information (for example, discriminating between key information and supporting detail).

The top-down approach to language processing bears many similarities to the pragmatic expectancy grammar developed by Oller (1979). Both models stress the importance of taking into consideration language and background knowledge in comprehending discourse. The link between our knowledge of language forms and our knowledge of the world has a number of implications for discourse processing. First, it suggests that the more predictable the sequences of language in a text, the more readily it will be understood. Texts for children learning to read should therefore be written in a style that is consistent with the children's oral language patterns. The phonics approach to reading presents children with more predictable language at the level of the word, but less predictable language beyond the word. A second way of exploiting the relationship between the world of the text and the world beyond the text is to ensure, not only that the linguistic elements are more predictable, but that the content is more familiar and therefore more predictable to the reader.

One of the criticisms that could be made of top-down processing as it is applied to the teaching of reading, is that it fails to distinguish adequately between beginning readers and fluent readers. Smith (1978) argues that, as fluent readers recognize words on sight, then this is how beginning readers should be taught. (He points out that children learning ideographic written systems such as Chinese learn in this way – that is, by recognizing the unique shape of each character.) However, it does not logically follow that, because fluent readers proceed mainly through sight recognition (assuming that they do), then this is the way that beginning readers should be taught.

3.4.3 Interactive processing

More recently, top-down processing has come in for some serious criticism. Stanovich (1980), in an exhaustive review of language-processing models, criticizes the notion that processing proceeds through making hypotheses and predictions about what might follow in the text and about content. Given problems with both bottom-up and top-down models, he proposes a third, which he calls the interactive-compensatory model. As the name indicates, this model suggests that, in comprehending discourse, we use information from more than one level simultaneously. In other words, comprehension is not a simple matter – either of moving from lower to higher, or from higher to lower elements – but is an interactive process.

This third model is superior to the two preceding it in several regards. The bottom-up model is deficient because it assumes that the initiation of higher-level processes (for example, making inferences) must await the completion of lower ones. The top-down model, on the other hand, does not allow lower-level processes to direct higher-level ones. There are also problems with the top-down suggestion that listeners/readers form hypotheses which they test out through the selective sampling of discourse elements.

In interactive models, deficiencies at one level can be compensated for by any other level, regardless of whether it is higher or lower in the hierarchy. For example, higher-level processes can make up for deficiencies at lower levels, and this allows for the possibility that readers with, say, poor reading skills can compensate for these by using other factors. These factors might include knowledge of the syntactic class of a given word or higher-level semantic knowledge. According to Stanovich, most top-down models do not allow for the possibility that less proficient readers may use higher-level processes to compensate for lower-level ones. He goes on to suggest that, given deficient decoding skills, poor readers may actually be more dependent on higher-level processes than proficient readers, a suggestion that is consistent with several empirical studies into reading comprehension.

3.5 Conversation analysis

Conversation analysts attempt to describe and explain the ways in which conversations work. Their central question is: 'How is it that conversational participants are able to produce intelligible utterances, and how are they able to interpret the utterances of others?' This type of analysis is rather different from other forms of discourse analysis, the differences stemming in part from the fact that it was developed within a sociological rather than linguistic tradition, the school itself being known by the rather intimidating term **ethnomethodology**. Interest in the analysis of conversation by scholars working in a number of different academic disciplines is hardly surprising as conversation is probably the basic form of communication. '. . . conversation is clearly the prototypical kind of language use, the form in which we are all first exposed to language – the matrix for language acquisition.' (Levinson 1983: 282)

Ethnomethodologists insist that data should be derived from naturally occurring instances of everyday interaction. In particular, they reject the use of data obtained through formal experiments, interviews and other forms of elicitation. This contrasts with other forms of discourse analysis (and, in fact, other social sciences where elicitation is a very common means of collecting data). In addition, they reject the use of invented speech samples, a practice favoured by certain schools of linguistics and applied linguistics. (They would therefore not admit as evidence texts such as those by Widdowson involving teapots, postmen and statistical probability.) In a key collection of papers on conversation analysis, Atkinson and Heritage (1984) point out that virtually none of the data in their book:

could conceivably be the product of recollection or intuition . . . by comparison with the richness and diversity of empirically occurring interaction . . . nor would such invented "data" prove persuasive as evidence relevant to the analysis of interaction. Data of this sort can always be viewed as the implausible products of selective processes involving recollection, attention or imagination . . . (p. 2)

They are also highly critical of the formal experiment as a research tool, arguing that the success of an experiment will depend on the extent to which the researcher has been able to limit, control and manipulate the behaviour in question. It is the researcher who decides before the event which behaviours are relevant and which are irrelevant. Yet the question remains as to where the variables came from in the first place. '. . . without previous exposure to a range of naturally occurring interactional data, the experimenter is unlikely to anticipate the range, scope, and variety of behavioural variation that might be responsive to experimental manipulation, nor will he or she be in a position to extrapolate from experimental findings to real situations of conduct.' (Atkinson and Heritage 1984: 2–3)

A characteristic feature of this type of research is the very elaborate analysis of relatively small samples of language. For example, Davidson (1984) investigates what happens in a conversation when an invitation, offer, request or proposal is rejected. Her database includes relatively short rejection sequences such as the following:

3x

A: I was gonna say if you wanted to you could meet me at UBC and I could show you some of the other things on the computer, maybe even show you how to program Basic or something.
B: Well, I don't know if I'd want to get all that involved.
A: It's really interesting.
(Adapted from Davidson 1984: 108)

Among other things, Davidson claims to have found that, following a rejection, speakers typically reformulate their offer, and that the subsequent version provides the interlocutor with an alternative which provides a **face-saving** way for the interlocutor to reject the offer.

Questions that conversation analysts have investigated include the following:

— How do topics get nominated, accepted, maintained and changed?
— How is **speaker selection** and change organized?
— How are conversational ambiguities resolved?
— How are non-verbal and verbal aspects of conversation organized and integrated?
— What role does intonation play in conversation management?
— What recurring functional patterns are there in conversation, and how are these organized?

'— How is socially sanctioned behaviour (for example, politeness versus rudeness, directness versus indirectness) mediated through language?

ACTIVITY

Study the following conversations. In what ways are the patterns of interaction different? Can you suggest how these differences might be accounted for?

3y

T: *What's it called?*

A: *Tools.*

T: *Tools. What's it going to be about? Can you tell me about it in your own words?*

A: *I, I wanna do a second draft with that one, and this one's done.*

T: *That is the second draft?*

A: *No, this is a different one.*

T: *A different story. Well, let's work on one of them first. Which one are you going to work on? Which one would you like to bring to the publishing . . .*

A: *This one.*

T: *That one. So really, that's your first draft, is it?*

A: *That's my second draft.*

T: *Well, come over here and let's see what this is. You reckon you've changed it, you've fixed up spelling and sentences and things?*

A: *I was reading – I was reading this one to Vlatko.*

T: *You've conferenced with a friend?*

A: *Yes.*

T: *And you've written it out, and now you want to conference with me. Well, I'll believe you. It's a shame you've lost other parts though. Read it to me please.*

A: *'Tools. Tools can help us use – to make houses or buildings and to fix things if they break. You need to make boats and cars and things. Cars and machines have' – supposed to be – 'lots of different things'.*

T: *Good. Fix it up then. Please don't disturb Daniella, as she is writing out her final copy. Try to write very quickly, Daniella, so it can go to the typist today . . . I think the word 'different' we've used lots of times . . . Spelling mistake! Go and fix it up.*

A: *Another spelling mistake.*

T: *Right. Now listen to this sentence and see what you think of it. 'You need to make boats and cars and machines and lots of different things.'*

A: *I have to add more.*

T: *Do you try to . . . Are you meaning to say you need <u>tools</u> to make boats and cars?*

A: *Yes.*

T: *I think you did mean that. 'You need tools to make boats and cars and machines and lots of different things.' You listen to this story as I read it to you and see what you would suggest to the writer. Let's pretend this is my story and I'm reading to you OK? 'Tools. Tools can help you to make houses or buildings and to fix things if they break. You need tools to make boats and cars and machines and lots of different things . . .' What would you suggest to me to do to make this story better?*

A: *Add more.*

T: *Add more? What else could I add, I can't think. What else could I add about, Alex?*

A: *What kinds of tools you need.*

(Author's data)

3z

A: *I rang to speak to Suzie last night and, ah, she was breastfeeding and I couldn't.*

B: *Are Suzie and Anna sisters?*

A: *Sisters, mmm, yeah.*

B: *So she's home from hospital?*

A: Yeah – she must've been for some time actually – the baby was born two weeks ago.

B: Oh, right . . . yeah, Robyn came home with all her gunk from the hospital . . . aaah cutbacks mean you have to – when you go into hospital – you have to take four dozen disposable nappies minimum, you have to take your own sanitary napkins, you have to take your own nipple pads, you have to take your own lanolin all of those things – they don't provide it . . . So I had my own babies just in time. I also filled up my case full.

C: Yeees, we also took . . .

B: . . . yes, and we were mild. There was this huge woman just down the way from me, a couple of bedrooms down, who, every time her husband came to visit her went off with a bagful of stuff – she was amazing.

A: No wonder they've had to impose cutbacks. (*laughter*)

B: I only took home things that I'd started like the tubes of lanolin that I'd started I threw in. (*mmm*)

A: Yeah.

B: Nigel came home in a hospital singlet (*laughs*). I thought that was really devilish . . . I was really upset when Mike took it back.

A: So this is the government's cuts presumably.

C: Uh-huh.

B: And the other thing is they're doing research on squatting techniques for giving birth . . . and they've asked Robyn if she would be in a . . . interested in being in the squatting group

A: God!

B: where they train you during your time . . .

A: . . . You'd have to learn to squat.

B: . . . to squat and give birth.

A: Somebody was telling me about a programme they'd seen where you . . . was it . . . a new birthing technique . . . squatting in a river on a stone or something or was it in the water.

B: Ah, the Russians did an in-the-water one . . . or they . . . they

A: Where . . . you're you're in the water or the baby drops into the water.

C: *You're supposed to (inaudible) . . .*

B: *No, you're in the water.*

A: *Be bloody cold.*

B: *Well, you'd be in warm water.*

C: *You'd be in warm water blood temperature.*

A: *No, this is a stream, a stream.*

B: *No, they do it, they have . . .*

A: *No, somebody, no somebody was telling me about a television programme or something and the . . . water would've been very cold . . .*

B: *That's the pygmies.*

A: *It was the pygmies, that's right.*

B: *The pygmies – I saw it.*

A: *Yeah.*

B: *Yeah, that's right.*

(Author's data)

In text 3y, which is from a discussion between a teacher and pupil about a piece of writing produced by the pupil, it is the teacher who controls the conversation in terms of the **topic**. She also decides who will speak. The second text (3z) is a casual conversation between friends, and the management of the conversation is, in consequence, very different. Notice the way that the general theme, that of childbirth, evolves – almost as a stream of consciousness through a number of different topics. The conversation is dominated by A and B who hold the floor most of the time. C makes one or two bids to contribute, but does not get very far. This might either be because she is a passive personality, or because she does not have children herself and therefore cannot claim authority over the topic in question.

3.6   Negotiating meaning

All but the most constrained interactions are the result of the joint efforts of the participants to make sense to each other. This is reflected in the amount of **negotiation** which is required in order for conversational participants to stay 'on track' – that is, for speakers to ensure that their messages are being received in the way they intended, and for the listeners to ensure that they are interpreting what they hear correctly.

ACTIVITY

Study the following pieces of interaction and identify the points at which the participants take steps to ensure that they are still discussing the same things. How do they achieve this?

3aa
A: *How do I get to Kensington Road?*
B: *Well you go down Fullarton Road . . .*
A: *. . . what, down Old Belair, and around . . .?*
B: *Yeah. And then you go straight . . .*
A: *. . . past the hospital?*
B: *Yeah, keep going straight, past the racecourse to the roundabout. You know the big roundabout?*
A: *Yeah.*
B: *And Kensington Road's off to the right.*
A: *What, off the roundabout?*
B: *Yeah.*
A: *Right!*
(Author's data)

3ab
A: *. . . the achitectural drawings will show us the elevations on the building. Do you know what I mean by elevations?*
B: *elevations, levels?, no*
(Willing 1992)

3ac
A: *it would be an elevation*
B: *Oh yeah front*
A: *from that elevation*
B: *Yeah, yeah, I understand*
A: *side elevation*
B: *Yeah*
(Willing 1992)

3ad
M: *Yes, but I mean, er, I agree, they all, erm, foremen. Supervisor, by the way, is the same to me. Isn't it to you?*
G: *Um, no, it's not quite the same thing to me. A foreman is, uh, somewhat lower on the, er, range, right?*
M: *All right, so he himself is not a supervisor and he is in the same rank as Geoffrey, yeah?*
G: *Yeah.*
M: *But they, they all three have some kind of leading operator or a foreman job right? We can't have a foreman doing a union job.*
G: *Well, actually, I must say on this issue that foreman are, in fact, um, key figures – usually in the union . . . the trade union setup.*
(Nunan 1991: 12)

In these extracts, there are numerous examples of the speakers and listeners doing conversational 'work' to ensure that there is mutual comprehension. In extract 3aa, the listener uses phrases such as the following to ensure that she has correctly understood the speaker: *. . . what, down Old Belair, and around . . .? . . . past the hospital? What, off the roundabout?* In extract 3ab, the speaker asks, *Do you know what I mean by elevations?* to ensure that the listener has correctly received his message. At other points in the extracts the listeners signal comprehension by using phrases such as: *Right! Yeah, yeah, I understand,* The final extract involves a native speaker and a second language learner, who are negotiating the meaning of the terms *supervisor* and *foreman* (the preceding discussion had been in danger of breaking down because the second language speaker was using the two terms synonymously).

The concept of meaning negotiation has become of interest to second language teachers and researchers in recent years. It has been argued that the second language acquisition process is enhanced by classroom tasks in which the learners are required to negotiate meaning (see, for example, Swain 1985). It is argued that when learners are put into a position where they have to negotiate meaning in order to make themselves comprehensible to their interlocutors, they will be pushed to the limits of their competence, and that this will 'fuel' the acquisition process. A number of researchers have spent the last few years experimenting with tasks of various kinds to determine which seem most appropriate. They have found that problem-solving and information gap tasks, in which learners are required to exchange and share information in order to complete the task, seem to stimulate the maximum amount of negotiation.

ACTIVITY

Identify the points of negotiation in the following exchanges involving native speakers (NS) and Non-native speakers (NNS).

3ae
NS: *And right on the roof of the truck, place the duck. The duck*
NNS: *I to take it? Dog?*
NS: *Duck.*
NNS: *Duck.*
NS: *It's yellow and it's a small animal. It has two feet.*
NNS: *I put where it?*
NS: *You take the duck and put it on top of the truck.*
(Pica, Young and Doughty 1987: 740)

3af

NS: So he wrote her a letter and explained that he was going to take a trip with Carol.

NNS: Eh?

NS: He wrote a letter to Diane, who was in Europe, and told her that he was planning to take a trip, with Carol, the woman he had just met.

NNS: I don't understand.

NS: Carol, you remember Carol?

NSS: One more time please.

(Rost and Ross 1991: 241)

3ag

NNS: There has been a lot of talk lately about additives and preservatives in food. In what ways has this changed your eating habits?

NS: Uh . . . well I guess it hasn't changed too much, uh, my eating habits. I try and avoid a lot of, uh, if it had preservatives or additives in it.

NNS: Pardon me?

NS: Pardon?

NNS: Pardon me, uh, what did you say?

NS: Oh, I said I, don't care too much whether it has additives or preservatives in, in the food itself, uh, as long as I'm eating somewhat, uh, balanced diet . . .

(Gass and Varonis 1985: 47–8)

3.7 Intercultural communication

A major challenge confronting second and foreign language users is to learn how to manage discourse processes in the target language. Researchers have shown that conversational dynamics and the performance of speech acts differ from language to language and culture to culture. Learning another language therefore involves much more than learning the pronunciation, vocabulary and grammar, although these things typically make up the bulk of foreign language programmes.

In addition to having different expectations about how to do things with language, learners from different cultures have very different types of background knowledge, and this can impede communication. A study by Steffensen (1981), for example, showed that when readers were exposed to written texts which described aspects of a culture foreign to them, there was a breakdown in comprehension.

Odlin (1989) provides a very useful survey of research into cross-linguistic comparisons of discourse. He argues that investigating discourse is more challenging than other areas such as phonology or syntax, but that it is a critically important area for applied linguistic research.

... when learners violate norms of conversation in the target language, the violations are potentially much more serious than syntactic or pronunciation errors since such violations can affect what is often termed "the presentation of self" ... Cross-linguistic differences in discourse may affect comprehension as well as production. A learner may interpret conversations and monologues in the target language in terms of native language norms, and may mistakenly believe that native speakers are being rude in situations where they are actually behaving appropriately according to the norms of their speech community. (Odlin 1989: 48–9)

Studies have been carried out into a number of different speech acts, including requests, apologies and greetings. All show considerable variation from one language to another. Variation is also evident in different societies that use English. On a recent trip to California, I observed the bemusement with which hotel guests from Britain received the standard *Missing you already!* which has replaced *Have a nice day!* as a farewell message from the front desk.

In addition to different speech acts, there are cultural differences in conversational management. Politeness, levels of formality, and the acceptability of stretches of silence all vary from culture to culture, and may have an important influence on the success or otherwise of a particular interaction. For example, in English, silence is only tolerated among individuals who know each other well, and when strangers or non-intimates meet, the participants work hard to ensure that there is a constant stream of talk. For Japanese speakers, this stream of talk can be disconcerting (Loveday 1982).

PROJECT

1. Record and analyse a 5–10 minute piece of casual conversation. Identify the following:
— topic selection and change
— the negotiation of meaning
— the speech acts that are performed
— techniques for keeping the interaction going (e.g. **back-channel feedback** in which the listener indicates that he or she is following the speaker by using terms such as *I see* and *Uh-huh*).
2. Reflect on the data collection exercise.
— What difficulties did you encounter?
— What did you learn about the nature of conversation?
— Compare your data with (a) conversations in a language teaching textbook (for example, *The Cambridge English Course*) and (b) conversational extracts from a modern play (for example, a play by Harold Pinter). What similarities/differences are there between the casual conversation, the textbook and the play?

SUMMARY

● Understanding discourse involves more than formal text-forming devices such as cohesion. It also involves using our background knowledge and our knowledge of context so as to understand the functions of individual sentences and utterances within the discourse.

- In order to understand how it is that humans are able to communicate successfully with one another, it is necessary to consider not only the words that appear on the page but also the knowledge and skills of the language users themselves.
- Schema theory attempts to explain how we use our background knowledge to comprehend discourse.
- In order to achieve mutual understanding, participants must negotiate meaning to ensure that they are being understood correctly, and that they are correctly interpreting the utterances of the other participants.

4 Developing discourse competence

4.1 The early years: oral competence

In this, the final chapter in the book, I shall look at the acquisition of discourse by both first and second language speakers. In comparison with the acquisition of grammar, discourse has been comparatively neglected by first and second language acquisition researchers, although this state of affairs is beginning to change. There has been some research into the acquisition of certain functional skills (such as the ability to refer to entities in the environment by using 'pointing' words such as *this* and *that*). The development of conversational competence by young children, and the role of the parent or primary caregiver, has also been investigated.

ACTIVITY

Analyse the following two conversations between a child and his mother (from Wells 1981). Look in particular for what the child has learned to do with language (that is, identify the functions of the child's utterances). In addition, identify the conversational techniques that the child has mastered, and examine the mother's contribution to the interactions. Finally, is there any evidence that the child's language has developed between the first and second texts?

4a
(Note: (*v*) = vocative, square brackets = inaudible, asterisk = indecipherable

what age?

Mark is looking in a mirror and sees reflections of himself and his mother.

1	Mark:	Mummy (v)	
2		Mummy	
3			Mother:	What?
4	Mark:	There – there Mark	
5			Mother:	Is that Mark?
6	Mark:	Mummy	
7			Mother:	Mm
8	Mark:	Mummy	
9			Mother:	Yes that's Mummy
10	Mark:	*	
11		Mummy	
12		Mummy (v)	
13			Mother:	Mm
14	Mark:	There Mummy	
15		Mummy (v)	
16		There. Mark there.	
17			Mother:	Look at Helen
18				She's going to sleep

(long pause)

Mark can see birds in the garden

19	Mark:	[ ] (= look at that)	
20		Birds Mummy (v)	
21			Mother:	Mm
22	Mark:	Jubs (birds)	
23			Mother:	What are they doing?
24	Mark:	Jubs bread	
25			Mother:	Oh look
26				They're eating the berries aren't they?
27	Mark:	Yeh	
28			Mother:	That's their food

29		They have berries for dinner
30	Mark:	Oh

4b

Mark has seen a man working in his garden

1	Mark:	Where man gone?	
2		Where man gone?	
3			Mother: I don't know
4			I expect he's gone inside because it's snowing
5	Mark:	Where man gone?	
6			Mother: In the house
7	Mark:	Uh?	
8			Mother: Into his house
9	Mark:	No	
10		No	
11		Gone to shop Mummy	

The local shop is close to Mark's house

12			Mother: Gone where?
13	Mark:	Gone shop	
14			Mother: To the shop?
15	Mark:	Yeh	
16			Mother: What's he going to buy?
17	Mark:	Er – biscuits	
18			Mother: Biscuits mm
19	Mark:	Uh?	
20			Mother: Mm
21			What else?
22	Mark:	Er – meat	
23			Mother: Mm
24	Mark:	Meat	

25		*Er – sweeties*	
26		*Buy a big bag*	
27			*Mother:* *Buy sweets?*
28	*Mark:*	*Yeh*	
29		*M – er – man – buy*	
		the man buy sweets	
30			*Mother:* *Will he?*
31	*Mark:*	*Yeh*	
32		*Daddy buy sweets*	
33		*Daddy buy sweets*	
34			*Mother:* *Why?*
35	*Mark:*	*Oh er – [ ] shop*	
36	*Mark:*	*Mark do buy some –*	
		sweets – sweeties	
37		*Mark buy some – um –*	
38		*Mark buy some – um –*	
39		*I did*	

Grammatically, the child's language is highly limited. Despite this, there is evidence that he has learned a great deal about how to carry on a conversation. In fact, in interactional terms, the conversation is remarkably similar to ordinary conversation. Mark is able to take turns appropriately, and is also capable of maintaining a particular conversational topic over several turns. Functionally, he is able to do the following things:

— initiate an interaction (see lines 1, 12 and 19)

— draw attention to what is currently of interest (see lines 6, 14 and 20)

— acknowledge his mother's contributions (lines 27 and 30).

The mother plays a very different conversational role from that which she would play in interaction with another adult. She interprets Mark's utterances to ensure that the interaction keeps going. She herself uses simple utterances and only talks about things in the here and now. She also 'leads from behind', allowing Mark to take the initiative. Through her conversational work, she is teaching Mark about the relationship between linguistic structures and objects and actions in the real world.

It is clear, in 4b, that Mark's language has developed. The length and complexity of his utterances have increased (see, for example, lines 1, 11, 26 and 36). In lines 17 and 22, we see him responding appropriately to information-seeking questions. In addition, he is able to talk about persons and events that are not present in the here and now.

The mother continues to play an important role in making the conversation work. She follows Mark's lead, despite his rejection of her suggestion that the man has gone inside because of the weather. She checks her understanding through **clarification requests** and **confirmation checks** in lines 12 and 14, and then assists Mark in building a fictional account involving a sweet shop. In fact the interaction owes as much to the structure provided by the mother as to Mark's contributions. The resulting story is achieved collaboratively between child and mother through a negotiation process which bears many similarities to adult conversation. The main difference lies in the contribution of the mother in interpreting what Mark is trying to say, in tailoring what she has to say to Mark's contributions, and in encouraging Mark to expand his own linguistic knowledge and skills.

While research such as this has shown that children learn discourse strategies such as **turn-taking** and **topic selection and change** early on, there are other aspects of discourse competence that are still being acquired well into the school years. (The above analysis is paraphrased from Wells 1981.)

ACTIVITY

Consider the following conversation between an adult (S) and a 7-year-old boy (R). What is problematic about the boy's side of the interaction?

4c
S: *Y'ever been fishing?*

R: *Nnnn my my cousins always goin fishin cuz they're/* lʊcki /(lucky)
for me. I cu'n go cuz I didn't know how t'fish. They're lucky go –
they go with my mom and my mommy and my – her sister's
father named Russell Magurry. Russell Magurariy. We call him
Magurburry.

S: *Uh-huh.*

R: *That's what we call him. But his real name is Russell.*

S: *Just like yours, huh?*

R: *Yeh, an y'know what?*

S: *What?*

R: *My fa–grandfather Russell, he lets us in the boat Saturday and*
Sunday, y'know what would we do? I'm not – when we taking a
day off, me and my mom and dad and Jess go to see my cousin
and then sometimes we stay there longer and sometimes we don't
cuz y'see we can – we went there before and first time when we's
gonna come to here but we hadda stay over there and we came we
went a LOT of places =

S: *Uh-huh*

R: *= slipped (slept) at night. And we hadda we – we hadda go at*
night and mornings until we finally got to Las Vegas, Nevada.
And then took a shortcut to here and then we shorted cut that
way to this rest area and he telled us go this way and then we
went to Los Angeles and came this kwa – this lady. And then I we
found Burbank and then we slipped in this hotel room and then we
found an apartment and we moved on here.

S: *Okay, let's let Peter tell a story.*

(Hatch 1983: 140)

As we have already seen, assumptions made by the speaker about
the state of knowledge of the hearer are crucial to the organization
and content of discourse regarding what to say and how to say it.
In the above example, we see a child who has mastered the
mechanics of interaction regarding turn-taking and so on, but who
fails to consider the amount of shared information that the listener

needs in order to interpret the interaction adequately. The extract shows that a 7-year-old child still has a great deal to learn about how to carry on a successful interaction by taking into consideration what the hearer can be assumed to know about the subject at hand.

ACTIVITY

The following conversation is between a mother and her young daughter Cynthia. Is Cynthia older or younger that the child in 4b? What does she know about carrying on a conversation? (Note: 'Anthony' is Cynthia's older brother.)

4d

C: *Mum, there's a bee on your head.*

M: *Is there? where?*

C: *Made you look you dirty chook* [chook = chicken]

A: *You're the chook that made her look.*

M: *It would be nice if I had a bee on my head. I'd . . . come on little bee.*

C: *It would sting ya. (laughs)*

M: *Would it? Might not.*

C: *D'ere Mum there's a lizard on your head. (laughs) It's a blue tongue on your head.*

F: *A blue tongue – where?*

M: *On my head, daddy.*

F: *Goodness!*

C: *Mum – mum, he's on your cheek now.*

M: *Oh, lovely lizard.*

C: *Er, I made you look you dirty chook. (giggles) Ma, what's the – Anthony, what's the other part?*

A: *You're the chook that made her look.*

M: *Where did you learn that?*

A: *From us.*

M: (*Chuckles*) *Oh, dear!*

C: *Mum, there's – mum there's a bee on your head.*

M: *A bee – on my head? Naughty bee, off you get. Here Cynth.*

C: *I made y' look y' dirty chook you're the one what – what . . .*

A: *What does this say Cynth?*

C: *. . . what made me look . . . A bee on your head, Mum there's a bee on your head. There's a bee on your head.*

M: *Off you get bee, off you go.*

C: *I made y' look y' dirty chook you're the one what made me look.* (*giggles*)

M: *Oh, you're a funny girl, aren't you?*

C: *No, I made y' look.*

M: *Do you say that to your friends at school?*

C: *No.*

M: *Why not?*

C: *There's a bee on your head mummy.*

M: *Off you get bee – shoo.*

A: *No, Cynthia, that won't work, y' know. You've said that too many times. You've got to say a different one. Say . . .*

C: *There's a tiger on your head.*

M: *Is there?*

A: *Do you know what – Cynth, do you know what's green and hairy and has two fangs and big blue eyes?*

C: *You.*

(Rees 1982)

In this extract, we see the child engaged in a game-like interaction with her mother and older brother. Notice the amount of repetition by the child, and the tolerance on the part of the mother toward the repetition. Notice, as well, the way that the mother allows the child to control the interaction. This extract provides an excellent example of the way in which imaginative and repetitive elements of language use both work together to extend the child's mastery of the language.

4.2 School years

Until comparatively recently, it was assumed that the acquisition of a first language was largely complete in the first three years of life. We now know that this is not true – many aspects of children's grammatical as well as discoursal ability continue to develop after they enter school. (This is illustrated in text 4c above.) In fact, as we shall see in this section, mastery of spoken and written discourse continues well into the secondary school years.

4.2.1 Speaking skills

Over the last ten years, there have been numerous calls for more formal attention to the development of listening and speaking skills in schools. In a major study carried out in Britain, Brown and Yule (1983b) investigated the speaking and listening skills of secondary school pupils. They found that while most pupils were able to use language for social purposes, they were much less skilled at using language for transactional purposes (that is, language used to get things done in the real world). In addition, the pupils were not particularly skilled at taking what Brown and Yule refer to as 'long turns' – that is, monologues in which the speaker is required to put together a coherent sequence of utterances. They provide the following example of a long turn. In it, an old man is reminiscing about how things were when he was young.

4e

there were + so very good houses rather old fashioned but quite good houses + with very big rooms and that + and these were sort of better class people + people with maybe + minor civil servants and things like that you know that had been able to afford + dearer rents and that in those days you know + + but the average working class man + the wages were very small + the rents would run from

anything from about five shillings to + seven shillings which was
about all they could've possibly afforded in those days . . .
(Brown and Yule 1983b: 17)

In this research, it was found that, while the ability to construct
long turns such as this is to a certain extent an individualistic skill
which will vary from person to person, it is not a skill that is
automatically acquired by native speakers. In fact, the ability to
produce discourse that extends beyond a limited number of utterances, and in which information is conveyed clearly, needs to be
consciously learned. It can also benefit from explicit teaching, and
should therefore form part of the school curriculum. The general
inability of young people to take part in long transactional turns in
which they are required to transfer information accurately has,
according to surveys of public and private employer groups, re-
sulted in a perception that school leavers are 'inarticulate' (Brown
and Yule 1983b).

ACTIVITY

In the next conversation, the young person, G, does demonstrate a
range of interactional skills. Make a list of these skills. How might
the fact that this is primarily a social rather than a transactional
encounter account for the skills exhibited by the speaker?

4f
G: *I watched that film last night + remember that + did you see it?*
H: *no I'm afraid I didn't + haven't got a television + what was +*
G: *it's eh + it was about eh + the assassination of + President*
    Carter + I think it was
H: *mm*
G: *aye it was him and you saw it was a good film + I watched it*
    all +
H: *what happened in it?*
G: *well eh you just saw the ashassina + assassination and there was*

somebody taking the part of what the man had done that got shot
him eh + that shot him and they were following all the things
and all that and then + eh this other man went and shot him
because he liked the President + and then after that it just ended
up that he got took to prison +
H: oh, I see
G: so it was good + +
(Brown and Yule 1983b)

The researchers provide the following interpretation of this piece of
interaction:

G chats on and on, interactionally very competently. She checks on her
listener's state of knowledge in her first utterance. When she finds that her
listener did not see the film which she wants to comment on, she tells her
what happened in it. Summarising and narrating the content of a film is a
cognitively very difficult task. If there were some overriding transactional
requirement here, the speaker would need to express what she is saying a
good deal more clearly, and her listener would probably keep on interrupt-
ing to check that she understood who was doing what to whom at any
given point in the summary. As it is, neither speaker nor listener comments
on the inappropriateness of talking about a film which recounts the
assassination of 'President Carter'. Similarly the speaker – and presumably
the listener as well – does not keep a very close control over the possible
referents, in the speaker's last long turn, of expressions like *the man, him,*
they, and all that, this other man, him, he, he. If the listener needed to, she
could probably work out who was being referred to at any given time,
given that she has any background knowledge of the events portrayed in
the film. It is important to realise that this lack of specificity in primarily
interactional speech generally does not matter. Neither speaker nor listener
needs to keep tight track of the detail. (Brown and Yule 1983b: 15)

4.2.2   Reading and writing skills

In a series of studies carried out at the Open University in Britain,
it was found that pupils between eight and thirteen are still gradu-

ally and steadily extending their ability to perceive cohesive relation-ships in school texts. This is important, if one accepts Chapman's (1982) claim that the perception of cohesion is a significant factor in successful reading performance. His research showed that pupils having high scores on standardized reading tests were also most able to perceive cohesive relationships in texts. Nunan (1982) also found a high correlation between general reading ability as measured by a standardized reading test and the ability of second-ary pupils to identify cohesive relationships in secondary school texts.

Numerous studies, of relevance to teachers, have been conducted into the perception of different types of textual relationships. These studies are critical in indicating the reading material most likely to succeed in school – in subjects as diverse as science, social studies and literature. In one of these studies, researchers found that mid-primary pupils had great difficulty identifying very basic and very simple anaphoric relationships (those marked by items such as pronouns). In the following sample, *John* and *He* form an ana-phoric relationship.

John was late for school. He came in with a note, and apologized to the teacher.

More recently, it has been shown that children comprehend best when the noun form, rather than pronouns or ellipsis, occurs in written discourse. In the case of our example above, comprehension would have been enhanced by using *John* rather than *He* in the second sentence. These studies show that the amount of information immediately available to the reader, and the load imposed on the reader's memory, are important factors in reading comprehension, and should be taken into consideration in creating teaching and testing materials. Further research confirmed that the amount and type of information, and the distance between cohesive relation-ships in discourse were significant factors in reading comprehen-sion. Dukta (1979) also found that the amount of information represented by an anaphoric reference item was a major factor in the comprehension of discourse. (We saw earlier that demonstratives such as *this* can represent lengthy stretches of discourse.)

Much of the research into the ability of pupils to understand written discourse has focused on the area of conjunction. There are at least two reasons for this. In the first place, cognitive psychologists have always been interested in the ability of children to understand logical relationships such as cause–consequence, in discourse. They are also interested in logical reasoning by children (although, of course, their focus of attention is on perception and reasoning rather than discourse). In addition, educational linguists believe that logical relationships of the type marked by conjunctions are important elements in school texts, and that the ability to comprehend these relationships is an important skill for those who need to read academic texts.

There are too many studies in this area to be reviewed in any detail here. I shall therefore restrict myself to summarizing some of the more important findings, focusing on those which are relevant for education.

1. There is a significant correlation between the ability to identify logical relationships marked by conjunction and overall reading comprehension.

2. There is also a significant difference in the difficulty of different types of conjunction.

3. The comprehension of **logical connectives** (that is, conjunctions such as *therefore* and *however*) is an important aspect in the development of logical thinking.

4. The perception of logical connectives is an important factor in success in reading science texts at the secondary level.

5. Logical relationships of the type marked by conjunctions are the most difficult of the cohesive relationships for junior secondary pupils to identify in school texts.

Another important group of studies explored the significance of the markers themselves – that is, the conjunctions – for the perception of logical relationships. In other words, are texts that contain explicit relationships more easily comprehended than those in which the relationships are implicit? In chapter 3, we looked in some detail at the controversy over whether the cohesive items actually 'create' the relationships, and came to the conclusion that they did not. In the following sentences, for example, the same logical relationship exists. However, in the first it is explicit, whereas in the second it is implicit.

4g

1. *Tomato seedlings should be planted in early spring. <u>However,</u> unless there is continuous hot weather, they will not bear fruit until late spring.*
2. *Tomato seedlings should be planted in early spring. Unless there is continuous hot weather, they will not bear fruit until late spring.*

It has been found that pupils have greater difficulty comprehending implicit than explicit relationships. In other words, 1 will be easier to comprehend than 2. This demonstrates that, while these cohesive markers do not create coherence in texts, they do facilitate comprehension.

At the college (tertiary) level, it has also been found that explicitness is significant in the comprehension of causal relationships, and that, as with junior readers, the adult reader's comprehension of explicitly stated information is reduced when the information is made implicit. On the other hand, Freebody and Anderson (1983), using texts in which the cohesion was 'downgraded' to varying degrees, found that the cohesive devices did not significantly affect comprehension (they investigated other types of cohesion in addition to conjunction). In other words, they found that the difficulty lies in the nature of the textual relationships themselves rather than in the cohesive devices that marked this information.

Wishart and Smith (1983) investigated the perception of logical connectives by secondary students in two types of texts – history texts and texts on everyday topics. They found that the relationships in the history texts were significantly more difficult to identify than those in the everyday texts. In other words, if readers are familiar with the content of a text, they can use their background knowledge to comprehend the logical relationships, whether or not these are explicitly marked. If the subject matter itself is unfamiliar, then the explicit markers may facilitate comprehension.

The most comprehensive study in the area is one carried out by Gardner (1977, 1983). He looked at the ability of 16,000 secondary students to comprehend connectives in science texts. The first part of the project was to identify the more commonly occurring logical connectives. This was done in a massive word count of textbooks used at the secondary level. Items were then used in the construction of a test battery. Gardner found that certain types of relationship were consistently more difficult than others. In commenting on this finding, Gardner remarked that:

There is probably no single explanation. We can see that the LR (logical reasoning) items are consistently difficult: the ability to carry out syllogistic reasoning using logical operators such as 'only if' or 'if' is obviously more difficult than the ability to use these terms correctly in sentences. Other difficulties are possibly the result of unfamiliarity; 'hence' and 'therefore' have similar meanings; the former is more difficult, and occurs less frequently in written material, and almost certainly in oral discourse as well. (Gardner 1983: 17)

All of these studies share one thing in common. They show that the ability to perceive relationships across sentence boundaries is an important skill which children need to acquire if they are to succeed in comprehending and producing the academic discourse of the classroom. It follows from this that instruction in such skills should form part of the school curriculum, and that all teachers should know something about the discourse of their chosen subject.

SUMMARY

- Children acquire certain discourse skills, such as turn-taking ability, very early.

- The contribution of the primary caregiver (usually the mother) is very important to the development of interactional discourse skills in the child.
- Certain oral discourse skills – such as the ability to take longer speaking turns and to convey factual information clearly – are not acquired until well into the school years.
- There is evidence that these skills could and should be explicitly taught.
- In the area of reading and writing, children need explicit instruction in comprehending and producing relationships in discourse.

Further reading

Chapter 1

Cook, G. 1989. *Discourse.* Oxford: Oxford University Press.
Cook shows how the study of spoken and written language can provide valuable insights for language teachers.

McCarthy, M. 1991. *Discourse Analysis for Language Teachers.* Cambridge: Cambridge University Press.
McCarthy describes and evaluates different models of analysis, and examines the relationship between discourse and the other linguistic systems – that is, grammar, vocabulary and phonology.

Chapter 2

Brown, G. and **G. Yule.** 1983. *Discourse Analysis.* Cambridge: Cambridge University Press.
Although this has been around for almost ten years, it provides one of the most detailed and accessible accounts of central aspects of discourse analysis.

Hatch, E. 1992. *Discourse and Language Education.* Cambridge: Cambridge University Press.
Another excellent book, this contains a wealth of data and numerous challenging reader tasks integrated into the text.

Chapter 3

Recent books by **Hatch** (1992) and **McCarthy** (1991), although rather different in their approaches, offer excellent introductions to the role of the language user in the construction and interpretation of discourse.

Chapter 4

Foster, S. H. 1990. *The Communicative Competence of Young Children.* London: Longman.
A recent book on the acquisition of discourse skills by young children.

Glossary

Note: This glossary includes some terms which are not dealt with in this text but which are important to the subject as a whole.

adjacency pairs In conversation, pairs of utterances that commonly co-occur – such as question–reply, introduction–greeting.
Example:
A: *Michael, I'd like you to meet Angela.*
B: *How do you do.*

anaphoric reference Within a text, two or more references to the same person, object or action – marked by some form of **pronominalization**.
Example: *The symphony was written in 1812. It is considered to be one of the finest in the repertoire of nineteenth century symphonic compositions.*

back-channel In conversations, the provision of **feedback** from the listener(s) to the speaker. The purpose of such feedback is to let the speaker know he or she is being attended to, and to encourage the speaker to continue. The feedback may be verbal or non-verbal (for example, head nodding).
Example:
A: *I went to Big W yesterday . . .*
B: *Uh-huh*
A: *. . . and bought one of those Italian market umbrellas.*

background knowledge The knowledge of the world which the reader or listener makes use of in interpreting a piece of spoken or written language.

bottom-up processing Decoding the smallest elements first, and using these to decode and interpret words, clauses, sentences and then whole texts.

cataphoric reference A form of **cohesion** in which the **proform** (the item used to stand in for the text referent) occurs first, and can only be interpreted with reference to the subsequent text.
Example: *I simply won't put up with <u>this</u>. All this <u>fighting and bickering</u>.*

classroom discourse Ths distinctive type of discourse that occurs in class-rooms. Special features of classroom discourse include unequal power relationships which are marked by unequal opportunities for teachers and pupils to nominate topics, take turns at speaking etc. The typical pattern of interaction is one in which the teacher asks a question to which he or she already knows the answer, one or more pupils respond, and the teacher evaluates the response.
Example: [The teacher circulates around the room, asking questions about train travel. The students all have copies of a train timetable.]

T: *Now . . . back to the timetable. Where do you catch the train? Where do you catch the train?*
    [She points to a student in the front row.]
S: *Keswick.*
T: *Yeah . . . Now – what time . . . what time does the train leave?*
Ss: *Nine. Nine o'clock. Nine pm. Nine pm. Nine am.*
T: [leans over a student and checks the timetable] *OK. Depart nine am.*
(Nunan 1991)

clarification request   see **negotiation of meaning**.

cleft structure A sentence in which the normal Subject + Verb + Object pattern is recast to give greater prominence to a particular element within the structure.
Example: *Catherine plays tennis.* → *It's tennis that Catherine plays.* (To emphasize that Catherine plays tennis rather than hockey or softball.) → *It's Catherine who plays tennis.* (To emphasize that Catherine, rather than Maria or Sophie, plays tennis.)

coherence The extent to which discourse is perceived to 'hang together' rather than being a set of unrelated sentences or utterances.

cohesion The formal links that mark various types of inter-clause and inter-sentence relationships within discourse.

Examples:
Identity relationship
A: *D'you know <u>Bill</u>?*
B: *Yeah, I met <u>him</u> at the Exeter conference.*
Logical relationship
I can't make it today. <u>However</u>, tomorrow's a possibility.

collocation The regular pattern of partnerships between words. For example, *lean* collocates with *meat* but *thin* does not.

communicative competence The ability to use language effectively to communicate in particular contexts and for particular purposes. Communicative competence is said to consist of four subsidiary components: grammatical competence, sociolinguistic competence, discourse competence, and strategic competence.

communicative event A piece of oral or written interaction, which contains a complete message. The 'event' itself may involve oral language (for example, a sermon, a casual conversation, a shopping transaction) or written language (for example, a poem, a newspaper advertisement, a wall poster, a shopping list, a novel).

comprehension check see **negotiation of meaning**.

confirmation request see **negotiation of meaning**.

conjunction A device for marking logical relationships in discourse. According to Halliday and Hasan (1976), there are four types of logical relationship in English: additive (marked by conjunctions such as *and*); adversative (marked by words such as *but* and *however*); causal (marked by words such as *because*); and temporal (marked by words such as *firstly*, *then*, *next*).

content (lexical) word A word that refers to a thing, quality, state, action or event. Content words contrast with **function words**, which indicate grammatical relationships. In the following example, the content words are underlined.
Example: *In the <u>morning</u>, we are <u>taking</u> the <u>flight</u> to <u>Narita</u>.*

context There are two types of context – linguistic and experiential. The linguistic environment refers to the words, utterances and sentences surrounding a piece of text. The experiential environment refers to the real-world context in which the text occurs. For example, 'sermons' typically occur in a 'religious ceremony' environment. Certain linguists, particularly systemic-functional linguists, argue that context and purpose determine the grammar and structure of the discourse.

conversation   An oral interaction between two or more people. The major focus of interest in recent years has been in the analysis and interpretation of casual conversation – that is, interactions carried out for social purposes, rather than for the exchange of goods and services.

conversational analysis   A type of analysis that aims to identify the principles enabling individuals to negotiate and exchange meanings. The central question addressed by conversation analysis is: how do conversations 'work'? Researchers avoid invented samples of language, using only authentic data and data obtained through elicitation or formal experiments.

co-operative principle   This was formulated by the linguistic philosopher Grice (1975), as a way of accounting for how people interpret discourse. The principle is expressed in terms of four maxims: the speaker should be truthful, brief, relevant and clear and the interlocutor, in turn, should assume that the speaker is following the four maxims.

deixis   Elements of discourse that 'point' the reader or listener to particular points in space or time.
Examples:
Put the boxes over <u>there</u>.
Leave the peppers under the grill until the skin is charred. <u>Now</u>, pop them into a plastic bag and let them sweat until the skins are soft and can be removed easily.

discourse   **communicative events** involving language in context.

discourse analysis   The functional analysis of discourse. Discourse analysis is sometimes contrasted with **text analysis** which focuses on the formal properties of language.

ellipsis   The omission of clauses, phrases or words which can be recovered from other parts of the discourse. As Halliday and Hasan point out, ellipsis does not occur in every situation in which the speaker or reader

must supply information from elsewhere in the discourse (because this would apply to practically every sentence or utterance) but only to those instances in which specific structural slots have been left unfilled.
Example:
A: *Is the car still in the garage?*
B: *Yes, it is.*

ethnomethodology   A branch of sociology which is concerned with the analysis and interpretation of everyday spoken interaction.

exchange   A basic interactional pattern identified by Sinclair and Coulthard in **classroom discourse**. An exchange consists of three functional **moves** – an opening move, an answering move and a follow-up move. These days, these three moves are more commonly known as initiation, response and follow-up or feedback.
Example:
T: *How many groups do we need?* (Initiation)
S: *Three.* (Response)
T: *Three. Very good.* (Feedback)

face-saving   An important principle which seems to underly a great deal of interpersonal interaction is the need to 'save face'. This is most commonly achieved by the use of indirect **speech act** strategies. For example, if a speaker wishes to invite someone out, but is afraid of a rebuff, he or she may avoid asking a direct question such as *Would you like to come out with me?*, asking instead, *Are you doing anything this evening?*, or, even less directly, *There's a great movie on at the Capri this evening.*

feedback   The provision of information to a speaker about the message he or she has conveyed. Neutral feedback simply informs the speaker that his or her message has been received. It may be verbal (*Uhuh!*, *Mmmm*) or non-verbal (for example, a nod of the head). Evaluative feedback provides the speaker with information on whether his or her message has been positively or negatively received. Once again, it may be verbal (*Great!*) or non-verbal (for example, a smile or a frown). (See also **back-channel**.)

frame theory   see **schema theory**.

functions   Another name for **speech acts** – that is, the things people do through language (for example, apologizing, complaining, instructing).

function word   see **content word**.

genre   A particular type of oral or written communication such as a narrative, a casual conversation, a poem, a recipe or a description. Different genres are typified by a particular structure and by grammatical forms that reflect the communicative purpose of the genre in question.

given/new   Any utterance or sentence can be said to contain given and new information. Given information is that which the speaker or writer assumes is known by the listener or reader. New information, on the other hand, is that which is assumed to be unknown. Given and new information will be reflected in the structure of sentences and utterances. Examples: *It is the cat which ate the rat.* (Given: Something ate the rat. New: The cat did the eating.) *What the cat ate is the rat.* (Given: The cat ate something. New: The rat got eaten.)

grammatical metaphor   The process of turning functions that would normally appear as verbs, into entities represented by nouns.

grammatical word   (also called function word, structural word) see **content word**.

ideational meaning   That aspect of an utterance which relates to information about objects, entities and states of affairs. In other words, the ideational meaning relates to what the utterance is about. It contrasts with the **interpersonal meaning** which is related to the attitudes or feelings of the speakers or writers.

illocutionary function   The function performed by an utterance or piece of language. The **illocutionary force** of an utterance can only be understood if we know the context in which the utterance occurs. Example: The statement *There's a dog out the back* could, depending on the context, be a description, a warning, an explanation, an invitation etc.

information structure   The ordering of elements within sentences and utterances according to (a) assumptions about the current state of knowledge of the listener or reader, and (b) elements which the speaker or writer wishes to **thematize**.

insertion sequence   A sequence of utterances separating an **adjacency pair**. In the following example, the question/answer adjacency pair is separated by a number of intervening utterances which constitute an insertion sequence.

Example:

Question: A: *How much was it?*

B: *Oh, you don't really want to know, do you?*

A: *Oh, tell me.*

A: *Wasn't cheap.*

A: *Was it a pound?*

Answer: B: *Pound fifty.* (Author's data)

interpersonal meaning   That aspect of an utterance which reflects the speaker's attitude towards the topic of the utterance.

lexical cohesion   This occurs when two words in a text are related in terms of their meaning. The two major categories of lexical cohesion are **reiteration** and **collocation**.

lexical density   The ratio of **content words** to grammatical or **function words** in a text.

lexical relationships   The relationships between the **content words** in a text. Example (In the following text, the underlined words have the lexical relationship of synonymy): *I gave Sally a <u>dictionary</u>. The <u>volume</u> cost me a fortune.*

lexical word   see **content word**.

locutionary force   The **propositional** (as opposed to functional or **illocutionary**) meaning of an utterance or statement.

logical connectives   **Conjunctions** such as *therefore* and *however*, which mark textual relationships such as causality.

modality   The dimension of an utterance which allows the speaker or writer to reveal his or her attitude towards (a) the **propositional** content or (b) the **illocutionary force** of an utterance. Modality is most commonly expressed through modal verbs, although there are other ways in which it can be expressed, as the following examples show.

Examples:

(a) Indicating attitude towards propositional content.

Proposition: *The vicar did it.*

Modalized statements: *The vicar <u>may have</u> done it. <u>They say</u> the vicar did it. The vicar <u>must have</u> done it. <u>Obviously</u>, the vicar did it. The vicar <u>undoubtedly</u> did it. <u>I'm sure</u> the vicar did it.*
(b) Indicating attitude towards illocutionary force.
Directive: *Clean the car.*
Modalized statements: *<u>I'd suggest</u> you clean the car. <u>You might like to</u> clean the car. <u>How about</u> cleaning the car? <u>I'd be grateful if you'd</u> clean the car. <u>Can</u> you clean the car this morning?*

move A basic interactional unit in **classroom discourse** identified by Sinclair and Coulthard. Three-part exchanges consist of three moves – an opening move, an answering move and a follow-up move. (For an example of these three types of move, see **exchange**.)

negotiation of meaning The interactional work done by speakers and listeners to ensure that they have a common understanding of the ongoing meanings in a discourse. Commonly used conversational strategies include comprehension checks, confirmation checks and clarification requests.
Examples
comprehension check (a strategy used by the speaker to ensure that the listener has understood correctly):
A: *The paper should go on the outside of the packet – <u>know what I mean?</u>*
B: *Mmm.*
confirmation request (a strategy used by the listener for confirmation that what he or she has just heard is correct):
A: *I saw a bank robbery a couple of weeks ago.*
B: *<u>A robbery?</u>*
clarification request (a strategy used by the listener for a more explicit formulation of the speaker's last utterance):
A: *Did y'see Theo last night? He was as pleased as a lizard with a gold tooth.*
B: *Sorry? <u>What do you mean by that exactly?</u>*

politeness Discourse strategies that enable the speaker or listener to save face in an interaction.

pragmatics The study of the way language is used in particular contexts to achieve particular ends.

proform   see **cataphoric reference**.

pronominalization   The process of substituting a pronoun for a noun phrase.
Example: *I saw the Fungs yesterday. They've just come back from Hong Kong.*

pronunciation   Pronunciation is an important part of the study of spoken discourse. Particularly interesting is the role of rhythm, stress and intonation. These serve many discourse functions, including the highlighting of important information, the signalling of given and new information, the indication of speaker attitude etc.
Example:
A: *Did you see? Your cat just ate a MOUSE.*
B: *No, it was a RAT that the cat ate.*
A: *I'm SURE it was a mouse.*
B: *Sorry, you're WRONG, it WAS a rat.*

proposition   A single statement about some entity or event.

propositional meaning   The formal meaning of an utterance without reference to its **function** within a discourse. Propositional or locutionary meaning contrasts with pragmatic or **illocutionary** meaning.
Example: Propositionally, the utterance *The window is open* is a statement about an entity – that is, a window. The illocutionary force of this utterance (which can only be recovered from the context in which it occurred) may be: a request (*It's awfully cold in here – would you mind shutting the window?*); a suggestion (A: *I can't get out of the room – the door is stuck fast.* B: *The window is open – why don't you climb out?*) and so on.

recount   A sequence of events, initiated by an introduction and orientation, and ending with a comment and conclusion.

reference   Those cohesive devices in a text that can only be interpreted with reference either to some other part of the text or to the world experienced by the sender and receiver of the text.

reiteration   A form of lexical **cohesion** in which the two cohesive items refer to the same entity or event. Reiteration includes: repetition, synonym or

near synonym, superordinate and general word. In the following example, the underlined words refer to the same entity.
Example: *I'm having terrible trouble with my <u>car</u>. The <u>thing</u> won't start in the morning.*

repair   The correction or clarification of a speaker's utterance, either by the speaker (self-correction) or by someone else (other correction). These repairs serve to prevent communication breakdowns in conversation.

rheme   see **theme**.

schema theory   A theory of language processing which suggests that discourse is interpreted with reference to the **background knowledge** of the reader or listener. (The differences between schema theory and **frame theory** are essentially technical. For further information, see Brown and Yule (1983).)

semantics   A study of the formal meanings expressed in language without reference to the context in which the language is used.

speaker selection   In conversation, the procedures through which it is determined who should 'hold the floor'.

speech act   The functional intention of an utterance.

structural word   (also called function word, grammatical word) see **content word**.

substitution   The use of **proforms** to represent earlier mentioned entities or events. There are three types of substitution: nominal, verbal and clausal.
Examples:
Nominal substitution
These apples are rotten. These <u>ones</u> are rotten too.
Verbal substitution
A: *Tomoko always studies at night.*
B: *So <u>does</u> Keiko.*
Clausal substitution
A: *Is Nigel <u>taking you to the movies</u>?*
B: *I think <u>so</u>.*

text   The written record of a **communicative event** which conveys a complete message. Texts may vary from single words (for example *Stop!*, EXIT) to books running to hundreds of pages.

text analysis   The analysis of formal features of text such as **cohesion**, **text structure** and so on. The focus is on formal rather than functional analysis, and the analysis generally involves little reference to the extra-linguistic context which gave rise to the text.

text-forming devices   Within a text, formal linguistic devices such as pronouns for making multiple references to entities, events and states of affairs.

text structure   This term is used to refer to the overall structure of different types of text as well as logical patterns within texts – for example, problem–solution.

thematization   The process of giving prominence to certain elements in a sentence or utterance by placing them at the beginning of the sentence or utterance. (See **theme**.)

theme   The initial element in a sentence or utterance which forms the point of departure. The remainder of the sentence or utterance is known as the **rheme**.
Examples:

Theme	Rheme
I	*went to town yesterday.*
DILLON, Mavis,	*dearly beloved sister of Doris and aunty of Michael . . .*
It	*was the cat that ate the rat.*

top-down processing   The use of **background knowledge**, knowledge of text structures etc. to assist in the interpretation of discourse.

topic   The subject matter of a text.

topic selection and change   The interpersonal procedures through which interlocutors negotiate and agree on a conversational topic, and the procedures through which the topic is subsequently changed.

transactional language   Language that is used in obtaining goods and services. Transactional interactions are contrasted with interpersonal interactions where the purposes are primarily social.

Examples:

Transactional interaction – goods

A: *Hello.*

B: *Hello. And what would you like?*

A: *Umm . . . I'd like to buy some chicken satay . . . is it the satay chicken?*

B: *Yes, there's chicken satays that you can have.*

A: *Ah, yes.*

B: *They're very nice.*

A: *Ah, could you show me?*

B: *Yeah.*

A: *Ah, this is chicken satay . . .*

B: *They look like that.*

A: *Ah, that's very nice. Can I have ah . . . seven pieces? Thanks.*

B: *Yes, mmmmm.*

A: *How much is it?*

B: *$10.65.*

A: *OK. Thank you.*

(Mah and Byrnes 1991: 19)

Transactional interaction – services

A: *Excuse me, when . . . when will the next train go to the . . . ah . . . Outer Harbour?*

B: *Outer Harbour. You got a train at four o'clock.*

A: *Four o'clock.*

B: *Four o'clock. Another twenty minutes on platform 7.*

A: *Seven. Thank you.*

B: *After the train . . . after the Gawler Central train.*

A: *Thanks a lot.*

(Author's data)

transcription   The written, verbatim record of spoken language.

turn   One speaker's utterance, bounded by the utterances of one or more other speakers.

turn-taking   The process by which opportunities to speak are distributed between two or more speakers. Rules for turn-taking differ in different cultural contexts.

References

Ackroyd, P. 1990. *Dickens*. London: Sinclair-Stephenson.

Atkinson, J. M. and J. Heritage (eds.) 1984. *Structures of Social Action: studies in conversational analysis*. Cambridge: Cambridge University Press.

Austin, J. 1962. *How to Do Things with Words*. Oxford: Oxford University Press.

Bartlett, F. C. 1932. *Remembering: a study in experimental and social psychology*. Cambridge: Cambridge University Press.

Bransford, J. and M. Johnson. 1972. Contextual prerequisites for understanding: some investigations of comprehension and recall. *Journal of Verbal Learning and Verbal Behaviour*, 11, 717–26.

Brown, G. and G. Yule. 1983a. *Discourse Analysis*. Cambridge: Cambridge University Press.

Brown, G. and G. Yule. 1983b. *Teaching the Spoken Language*. Cambridge: Cambridge University Press.

Cambourne, B. 1979. How important is theory to the reading teacher? *Australian Journal of Reading*, 2, 78–90.

Cataldi, L. 1990. *The Women Who Live on the Ground*. Victoria: Penguin.

Chafe, W. 1990. Looking Ahead. *Text*, 10, 19–22.

Chapman, J. 1982. A study in reading development: a comparison of the reading ability of 8, 10, and 13 year old children to perceive cohesion in their school texts. Paper presented to the Nineteenth Annual Conference of the United Kingdom Reading Association, Newcastle-upon-Tyne.

Christie, F. 1989. Genres of writing. In *Writing in Schools* (B.Ed. Course Study Guide). Geelong, Victoria: Deakin University Press.

Cicourel, A. 1973. *Cognitive Sociology: language and meaning in social interaction*. Harmondsworth: Penguin.

Clyne, D. 1991. Photographing small beasties. *The Bulletin*, 24–31 December 1991.

Cook, G. 1989. *Discourse*. Oxford: Oxford University Press.

Cook, P. 1991. Not the news. *The Bulletin*, 24–31 December 1991.

Crystal, D. 1992. *Introducing Linguistics*. London: Penguin.

Davidson, J. 1984. Subsequent versions of invitations, offers, requests, and proposals dealing with potential or actual rejection. In J. M. Atkinson and J. Heritage (eds.) *Structures of Social Action: studies in conversational analysis*. Cambridge: Cambridge University Press.

Dutka, J. 1979. Anaphoric relations: comprehension and readability. Paper presented at the Annual International Conference on the Processing of Visible Language, Niagra-on-the-Lake.

Economou, D. 1986. *Coffeebreak: the language of casual conversation*. Adelaide: National Curriculum Resource Centre.

Edmonson, W. 1981. *Spoken Discourse: a model for analysis*. London: Longman.

Foster, S. H. 1990. *The Communicative Competence of Young Children*. London: Longman.

Freebody, P. and **R. Anderson**. 1983. Effects of vocabulary difficulty, text cohesion and schema availability on reading comprehension. *Reading Research Quarterly*, 18, 277–94.

Freeman, D. 1992. Collaboration: constructing shared understandings in a second language classroom. In D. Nunan (ed.) *Collaborative Language Learning and Teaching*. Cambridge: Cambridge University Press.

Gardner, P. L. 1977. Logical connectives in science. A Report to the Education, Research and Development Committee, Commonwealth Government, Canberra.

Gardner, P. L. 1983. Students' difficulties with logical connectives. *Australian Journal of Reading*, 6, 12–18.

Gass, S. and **E. Varonis**. 1985. Variation in native speaker speech modification to non-native speakers. *Studies in Second Language Acquisition*, 7, 37–58.

Grice, H. P. 1975. Logic and conversation. In P. Cole and J. Morgan (eds.) *Syntax and Semantics, Volume 9: Pragmatics*. New York: Academic Press.

Halliday, M. A. K. 1985a. *An Introduction to Functional Grammar*. London: Edward Arnold Publishers Ltd.

References

Halliday, M. A. K. 1985b. *Spoken and Written Language.* Victoria: Deakin University Press. (Also published in Oxford, 1989, by Oxford University Press.)

Halliday, M. A. K. and **R. Hasan**. 1976. *Cohesion in English.* London: Longman.

Hatch, E. 1983. *Psycholinguistics: a second language perspective.* Rowley, Mass.: Newbury House.

Hatch, E. 1992. *Discourse and Language Education.* Cambridge: Cambridge University Press.

Hoey, M. 1983. *On the Surface of Discourse.* London: Allen and Unwin.

Hoey, M. 1991. *Patterns of Lexis in Text.* Oxford: Oxford University Press.

Kintsch, W. and **J. Keenan**. 1973. Reading rate and retention as a function of the number of propositions in the base structure of sentences. *Cognitive Psychology*, 5, 257–74.

Levinson, S. 1983. *Pragmatics.* Cambridge: Cambridge University Press.

Loveday, L. 1982. Communicative interference: a framework for contrastively analysing L2 communicative competence exemplified with the linguistic behaviour of Japanese performing in English. *International Review of Applied Linguistics*, 20, 1–16.

McCarthy, M. 1991. *Discourse Analysis for Language Teachers.* Cambridge: Cambridge University Press.

Mah, D. and **F. Byrnes**. 1991. *Communicating: a teacher's guide.* Sydney: National Centre for English Language Teaching and Research.

Marr, D. 1991. *Patrick White: a life.* Sydney: Jonathon Cape.

Martin, J. R. 1981a. Conjunction: the logic of English text. Mimeograph, Linguistics Department, University of Sydney.

Martin, J. R. 1981b. Lexical cohesion. Mimeograph, Linguistics Department, University of Sydney.

Martin, J. R. 1984. Language, register and genre. In *Children's Writing: Reader.* Geelong, Victoria: Deakin University Press.

Mordden, F. 1980. *A Guide to Orchestral Music.* New York: Oxford University Press.

Nunan, D. 1982. The perception of inter- and intra-sentential semantic relationships in science and fiction texts by L1 and L2 (phase 2) secondary students. Research Report to the School of Education, Flinders University of South Australia.

Nunan, D. 1989. *Understanding Language Classrooms.* London: Prentice Hall.

Nunan, D. 1991. *Language Teaching Methodology: a textbook for teachers.* London: Prentice Hall.

Nunan, D., S. Hood and **J. Lockwood.** 1992 (pilot edition 1991). *The Australian English Course. Level 2.* Cambridge: Cambridge University Press.

Odlin, T. 1989. *Language Transfer.* Cambridge: Cambridge University Press.

Oller, J. 1979. *Language Tests at School.* London: Longman.

Pearson, I. 1978. *English in Biological Science.* Oxford: Oxford University Press.

Pica, T., R. Young and **C. Doughty.** 1987. The impact of interaction on comprehension. *TESOL Quarterly*, 21, 737–58.

Rees, D. 1982. Child language analysis. Unpublished monograph. Sturt College of Advanced Education, Adelaide, South Australia.

Richards, J., J. Hull and **S. Proctor.** 1990. *Interchange: English for International Communication, Student's Book 1.* Cambridge: Cambridge University Press.

Rost, M. and **S. Ross.** 1991. Learner use of strategies in interaction: typology and teachability. *Language Learning*, 41, 2, 235–73.

Searle, J. 1969. *Speech Acts.* Cambridge: Cambridge University Press.

Sinclair, J. McH. and **M. Coulthard.** 1975. *Towards an Analysis of Discourse: the English used by teachers and pupils.* Oxford: Oxford University Press.

Smith, F. 1978. *Understanding Reading.* New York: Holt, Rinehart and Winston.

Stanovich, K. E. 1980. Toward an interactive-compensatory model of individual differences in the development of reading fluency. *Reading Research Quarterly*, 16, 32–71.

Steffensen, M. 1981. Register, Cohesion and Cross-cultural Reading Comprehension. Technical Report No. 220. Centre for the Study of Reading, University of Illinois, Champaign, Illinois.

Swain, M. 1985. Communicative competence: some roles for comprehensible input and comprehensible output in its development. In S. Gass and C. Madden (eds.) *Input in Second Language Acquisition.* Rowley, Mass.: Newbury House.

References

Swales, J. 1990. *Genre Analysis*. Cambridge: Cambridge University Press.

van Dijk, T. 1977. *Text and Context: explorations in the semantics and pragmatics of discourse*. London: Longman.

Warshawsky, D. 1992. *Spectrum: a communicative course in English*. Englewood Cliffs, NJ: Prentice Hall.

Wells, G. 1981. *Learning Through Interaction*. Cambridge: Cambridge University Press.

Widdowson, H. G. 1978. *Teaching Language as Communication*. Oxford: Oxford University Press.

Widdowson, H. G. 1983. *Learning Purpose and Language Use*. Oxford: Oxford University Press.

Willing, K. 1992. *Talking it through: clarification and problem solving in professional work*. Sydney: National Centre for English Language Teaching and Research.

Wishart, E. and L. Smith. 1983. Understanding of logical connectives in history. *Australian Journal of Reading*, 6, 19–20.

Wolfe, T. 1979. *The Right Stuff*. New York: Farrar, Straus and Giroux.

Index